Praise for Diane Sweeney's
Student-Centered Coaching: A Guide for K–8 Coaches and Principals

Sweeney's stories of coaching and the useful materials, tips, and protocols bring student-centered coaching alive. This book has the power to revolutionize the ways coaching is conceptualized and enacted in K–12 schools nationwide.

—Nancy Fichtman Dana, Professor of Education
University of Florida School of Teaching and Learning
Gainesville, FL

Student-Centered Coaching will change the conversation about coaching in this country. For too long, coaches and principals have been angst-ridden about getting teachers to utilize certain teaching practices with precious little conversation about the outcome for students. Sweeney shows us how vital it is to focus our coaching efforts on the ultimate beneficiary—the student. With a myriad of tools including rubrics coaches can use to place themselves on the continuum of student-centered coaching, we walk away from this book with the means to implement student-centered coaching as well as an entirely different perspective.

—Ellin Oliver Keene, Author and Consultant
Mosaic of Thought (Heinemann, 1997)
Denver, CO

The breadth and depth of her knowledge led me to want to dig deeper and improve my coaching skills, and to advocate for student-centered coaching districtwide. She provides insight that I believe will impact my ability to get into more classrooms, to work more effectively with more teachers, and to be more thoughtful in my work.

—Mary L. Morris, Instructional Coach for Math & Science
Tacoma Public Schools
Tacoma, WA

An excellent resource that should be on the bookshelf of every principal and instructional coach.

—Roberto Pamas, Principal
O.W. Holmes Middle School
Fairfax County Public Schools
Alexandria, VA

This book is a must-have for new instructional coaches. I wish I would have had it at the beginning of my first year!

—Kevin Schlomer, Instructional Coach
Terrace Elementary School
Ankeny Community School District
Ankeny, IA

Diane has taken a commitment to instructional leadership and turned it into practical models and applications. She has a thorough grounding in the research, which she combines with extensive personal experience and a brass-tacks orientation toward helping teachers, coaches, and administrators improve.

—Rob Stein, Past Principal
Manual High School
Denver, CO

This is a timely and important piece in the coaching world. The focus on students rather than teachers is the only way we will help schools reach meaningful change.

—Jennifer Thoma, Instructional Coach
Northeast Elementary School
Ankeny Community School District
Ankeny, IA

STUDENT-CENTERED COACHING

A Guide for K–8 Coaches and Principals

DIANE SWEENEY

CORWIN
A SAGE Company

For information:

Corwin
A SAGE Company
2455 Teller Road
Thousand Oaks, California 91320
(800) 233-9936
Fax: (800) 417-2466
www.corwin.com

SAGE Ltd.
1 Oliver's Yard
55 City Road
London EC1Y 1SP
United Kingdom

SAGE India Pvt. Ltd.
B 1/I 1 Mohan Cooperative
    Industrial Area
Mathura Road, New Delhi 110 044
India

SAGE Asia-Pacific Pte. Ltd.
33 Pekin Street #02-01
Far East Square
Singapore 048763

Printed in the United States of America

Library of Congress Cataloging-in-Publication Data

Sweeney, Diane.
Student-centered coaching: a guide for K-8 coaches and principals/Diane Sweeney.
    p. cm.
Includes bibliographical references and index.
ISBN 978-1-4129-8043-2 (pbk.)
   1. Mentoring in education—United States. 2. Academic achievement—United States. 3. School improvement programs—United States. 4. Education (Elementary)—United States. I. Title.

LB1731.4.S87 2011
371.102—dc22   2010038705

This book is printed on acid-free paper.

16 17 18 19 12 11 10 9

Acquisitions Editor:	Dan Alpert
Editorial Assistance:	Sarah Bartlett
Production Editor:	Amy Schroller
Copy Editor:	Brenda Weight
Typesetter:	C&M Digitals (P) Ltd.
Proofreader:	Eleni-Maria Georgiou
Indexer:	Nara Wood
Cover Designer:	Michael Dubowe
Permissions Editor:	Karen Ehrmann

Contents

Acknowledgments

I began writing this book in the lazy days of summer. I would set up my computer just inside the screen door so I could hear the hummingbirds buzzing around. Now, with the project in its final days, winter has arrived and snow blankets the ground. At times the writing was a long, hard slog and at others my fingers seemed to light the keyboard on fire. Through the good and bad, through the hard and easy, the common thread has been the people that fill both the pages in this book and in my life. People whom I would like to thank.

First is Dan Alpert, Senior Acquisitions Editor for Corwin. Without Dan's interest and attention, this book simply wouldn't be.

Many thanks to a tireless group of district leaders, including Tony Byrd and Lara Drew (Edmonds School District, WA); Lisa Meredith (Parkway School District, MO); Cheri Patterson, Brian Shindorf, and Jaime Dial (St. Joseph School District, MO); Phil Collins and Amy Rubin (Glenview District 34, IL); Kathy Horvath (Northbrook District 28, IL); Carrie Cahill (Midlothian School District, IL); and Margo Mann (Wentzville School District, MO). I have benefited greatly from the insight, experience, and dedication of each of you.

I would like to thank the committed coaches and principals whom I have been privileged to work with. Too numerous to name, they include the coaches and principals from the following school districts: Edmonds (WA), St. Joseph (MO), Parkway (MO), Glenview 34 (IL), Northbrook 28 (IL), Midlothian (IL), Kent (WA), Federal Way (WA), and Wentzville (MO). A few whom I'd like to highlight are Julia Andrews, Maggie Conners, Kim Copeland, Shelly Dearmon, Pam Schaff, Marie Verhaar, Mary Sue Smith, Jamie Downes, Angie Klaassen, and Lisa Elifrits.

Many thanks to the teachers that I have learned alongside—teachers who have helped me detangle my thoughts about school-based coaching and figure out how it looked in *real* classrooms with *real* kids. Two that I would like to thank by name are Kristi Welch and Nicole Miller.

Thank you to Roberta Buhle, Shari Frost, and Marcia Caulkins at National Louis University. Your willingness to share my drafts in your coaching courses provided invaluable feedback and support.

I am indebted to Susan Levy, Mariah Dickson, Shannon Stanton, and Brooke O'Drobinak. I turned to you for insight and you tackled my messy and sometimes incoherent drafts with vigor. I thank you for taking time out of your busy lives to share your thoughts and opinions to make this a better book.

I sometimes wonder aloud when life will slow down, and then my husband reminds me that with a four-year-old and seven-year-old, it could be awhile. Many thanks to our family and friends who have brought to life the saying, "It takes a village." This includes Ted and Genese Sweeney, Richard and Karen Rosenberg, Kenneth Rosenberg, Gretchen Faber, and Cary Cazzanigi. Without them, I would have never been able to write this book.

To my children, who think it's really cool that I go off to work in classrooms and schools around the country. Their patience and love is without measure. And to my husband Dan, who, due to my many frequent-flier miles, has endured countless nights alone with our children, making a frozen pizza, giving baths, and tucking them in to bed. He truly understands the passion and importance I feel for this work and has supported me every step of the way.

The seasons will change once again, and our teachers and students will continue on with the important work that they do each and every day. And for them, I give thanks.

Publisher's Acknowledgments

Corwin gratefully acknowledges the contributions of the following reviewers:

Deborah Ekwo, Instruction Coordinator/Coach
Houston Independent School District
    Professional Development Services
Houston, TX

Kathy Ferrell, Instructional Coach
Excelsior Springs Middle School
Liberty, MO

Sandy Humbyrd, Math & Science Instructional Coach
Hollister R-5 Schools
Hollister, MO

Jenny Jacob, Instructional Coach
Ashland Ridge Elementary School
Ankeny, IA

Alissa Jones, Instructional Coach
Ankeny Schools
Ankeny, IA

Nicole Kemp, Principal
Williamsburg Elementary School
Williamsburg, MO

Marianne Lescher, Principal
Kyrene de la Mariposa Elementary School
Gilbert, AZ

Wanda Lofton, Instruction Services School Coach
John Stanford Center
Seattle, WA

Kristi Mixdorf, Instructional Coach
Northwest Elementary School
Ankeny, IA

Sara Muller, Instructional Coach
Westwood Elementary School
Ankeny, IA

Roberto Pamas
O.W. Holmes Middle School
Dallas, TX

Lois Reitz, Instructional Coach
South Valley Middle School
Gilcrest, CO

Linda Robinson, Retired Principal/School Consultant & Coach
Houston, TX

Ed Sansom, Principal
Seven Oaks Middle School
Lebanon, OR

About the Author

 **Diane Sweeney** is Lead Consultant for Spark Innovation, a consulting firm specializing in coaching, literacy, and leadership. In her current role, Diane supports teachers, coaches, principals, and district leaders in the development of a student-centered approach for instruction and professional development. Diane has also served as a teacher, literacy coach, and university professor. She currently lives with her family in Denver, Colorado.

Introduction

Why This Book? Why Now?

For over a decade, I have been fortunate to work with teachers, coaches, principals, and district leaders from around the country. And through this work, I have watched coaching evolve from a cutting-edge innovation in the early 90s to a common set of practices that exist in many of our schools today.

Though many educators will gladly testify to the benefits of school-based coaching, questions still persist about its effectiveness. I regularly meet many coaches who fret about their impact. They worry that, though they are very busy, they aren't quite sure how their daily effort is making a difference with students.

Student-Centered Coaching seeks to answer this question by introducing a new way of looking at and delivering school-based coaching that puts the needs of students front and center. By focusing coaching on specific goals for student learning, rather than on changing or fixing teachers, a coach can navigate directly toward a measurable impact and increased student achievement. Coaches are still busy, but now their efforts are targeted and aligned toward student learning.

Principals have been almost entirely overlooked with regard to coaching, yet without their leadership, coaching will fail to show the results we are hoping for. As the first book written with both coaches and principals in mind, you'll find a series of tools that are designed to foster dialogue, problem solving, and collaborative planning so that a principal and coach can work together to design and implement a student-centered coaching model.

Who Am I?

My journey began as a classroom teacher in an urban elementary school in Denver, Colorado. It was the early 1990s, and with one year of teaching under my belt and a class full of second-language learners, I was in over my head. But through my school's partnership with the Public Education & Business Coalition (PEBC), an educational nonprofit based in Denver, I was provided with the support I needed from a literacy coach . . . an experience that saved my life as a teacher. It was this experience that led me to write *Learning Along the Way: Professional Development By and For Teachers* (Stenhouse, 2003) and also motivated me to spend the past eleven years working to develop systems of support for teachers so that our schools can become a place where we come together and think deeply about how to best address our students' needs as learners.

How to Use This Book

One of my favorite things about this book is the diverse array of educators that fill its pages. You will read about school districts that are rural, urban, suburban, large, small, and somewhere in between. You will be introduced to school-based coaches who support literacy, math, science, and the humanities. And you will hear many examples of how principals are leading coaching in their schools. This rich array of individuals and perspectives shares a refreshingly simple goal . . . to increase the achievement of the students in their schools. And therefore provides the text with an overarching perspective that on first glance may be complex but when unpacked, is surprisingly straightforward and achievable.

It is important to keep in mind that no two schools are alike in terms of school culture, student population, and teacher demographics. And for that reason, this book is not meant to be implemented as a "program." But rather, I encourage you to come together as a team around the concepts, theories, and practices in an open and thoughtful way. You will find more success by customizing and tinkering with the ideas and tools to make them work in your own setting.

The book is organized into three sections. The first section defines student-centered coaching and explores key factors for establishing a coaching effort that is driven by student learning. Chapter 1 defines student-centered coaching and provides key practices for focusing coaching on student learning. Chapter 2 provides the steps for getting student-centered coaching up and running in your own school or district. And Chapter 3 speaks to the importance of establishing a learning culture in conjunction with a coaching effort.

Section Two explores the role of data and student evidence as it relates to coaching. Chapter 4 provides examples of how schools can draw upon student evidence in professional development and coaching. Chapter 5 explores strategies and tools for evaluating the impact that coaching makes on teachers and students.

The last section includes a variety of practices that underlie a student-centered coaching effort. Chapter 6 introduces classroom observations that are grounded in student evidence. Chapter 7 defines the systems and structures that contribute to a professional development model that is student-centered. Chapter 8 explores how we can engage adult learners while taking into account factors such as career stage, gender, and generation. And Chapter 9 provides insight into how districts can develop systems of support for coaches.

In her book *Turning to One Another* (2002), Margaret Wheatley writes, "I've seen that there is no more powerful way to initiate significant change than to convene a conversation" (p. 22). It is my hope that this book will inspire you to talk with one another and, in turn, reach the goals that you have for your students and teachers. Let's get the conversation started . . .

Section I

Establishing Student-Centered Coaching

1

The Next Generation of Coaching . . . Coaching Student Learning

Most educators are in agreement that the goal of school-based coaching is to improve student learning by providing continuous, relevant, and job-embedded support to teachers. But now that coaching is firmly rooted in many of our schools, and becoming newly established in others, we have to wonder about its impact. We have to consider whether coaching is improving student learning as we had hoped it would. And if it hasn't, we have to reconsider the approach we've taken thus far so we can ensure that coaching impacts our students in meaningful ways.

What Is Student-Centered Coaching?

Student-centered coaching is about (1) setting specific targets for students that are rooted in the standards and curriculum and (2) working collaboratively to ensure that the targets are met. Rather than focusing on how teachers feel or on the acquisition of a few simple skills, we measure our impact based on student learning.

Coaching often centers exclusively on the actions taken by the teacher—making the assumption that if we improve the teaching, then student learning will improve as well. There is some logic to this approach, but unfortunately an unintended outcome is we've spent so much time thinking about what teachers *should* be doing that we've lost touch with the most important people in our schools . . . the students.

As a leader in the field of professional development, Thomas Guskey has argued for a more student-centered approach for close to two decades. He writes, "In most cases, program effectiveness is judged by an index of participants' satisfaction with the program or some indication of change in their professional knowledge. Rarely is change in professional practice considered, and rarer still is any assessment of impact on student learning" (1995, p. 116). It's time to rethink how we define coaching and put our students front and center.

A Natural Connection to Formative Assessment

As an educator, you no doubt understand that teaching is about applying the curriculum in a way that best addresses the needs of any given group of students. Achieving this depends on the identification of (1) what the students know; (2) what the standards, curriculum, or program deems they need to know; and (3) how to design and implement instruction to meet these needs. Achieving this requires educators to formatively assess students and adjust the instruction accordingly. On paper this may sound simple, but in practice that is far from the case. It is a complex process that requires the following knowledge:

- Teachers understand how to apply a variety of methods, techniques, and strategies to formatively assess students throughout their learning.
- Teachers have a well-developed knowledge of the standards and curriculum they teach.
- Teachers draw from a deep well of instructional strategies and practices to promote student learning.

Formative assessment is a core element of student-centered coaching because it helps teachers understand how to use student evidence to drive their decision making and meet the students' needs. In their seminal work on formative assessment in the mid-1990s, Wiliam and Black (1996) write, "In order to serve a formative function, an assessment must yield evidence that, with appropriate construct-referenced interpretations, indicates the existence of a gap between actual and desired levels of performance, and suggests actions that are in fact successful in closing the gap." They further note that "all assessments can be summative, but only some have the additional capability of serving formative functions" (p. 543). W. James Popham concurs and through his work with the Council of Chief State School Officers (CCSSO) has come to define formative assessment as follows: "Formative assessment is a process used by teachers and students during instruction that provides feedback to adjust ongoing teaching and learning to improve students' achievement of intended instructional outcomes" (2008).

Can most teachers accomplish this alone? Of course there is a population of teachers who can, but there are many more who struggle to fit the pieces together in a way that helps students reach their full potential. These are the teachers who benefit the most from student-centered coaching.

Student-Centered vs. Teacher-Centered Coaching

As we navigate the coaching landscape, it is clear that the journey is different with each and every teacher. For this reason alone, we can't think about student-centered coaching in black-and-white terms, but instead as a continuum of student centeredness. The more student centered we are in our coaching work, the greater the impact will be on our students. The following figure compares student-centered coaching with a more traditional, teacher-centered model. Several key practices are highlighted that will be explored with others throughout this book (Figure 1.1).

Figure 1.1   A Continuum of Student-Centeredness in School-Based Coaching

More Impact on Student Learning		Less Impact on Student Learning
◄───►		
Student-Centered Coaching	*Teacher-Centered Coaching*	*Relationship-Driven Coaching*
Focus is on using data and student work to analyze student learning and collaborate to make informed decisions about instruction.	Focus is on what the teacher is or is not doing and addressing it through coaching.	Focus is on providing support to teachers in a way that doesn't challenge or threaten them.
District curricula or programs are viewed as tools for reaching student learning objectives.	Implementing a specific curriculum or program is viewed as the primary objective of the coaching.	District curricula or programs are a part of the conversation and are shared as possible resources for teachers.
Trusting, respectful, and collegial relationships are a necessary component for this type of coaching.	Trusting, respectful, and collegial relationships are a necessary component for this type of coaching.	Congenial relationships are more common for this type of coaching.
Coach is viewed as a partner that supports the teacher to meet his or her goals for students.	Coach is viewed as a person who is there to hold teachers accountable.	Coach is viewed as a friendly source of support.

Framing Coaching Around a Goal for Student Learning

Recently I had the opportunity to coach Kristi, a language arts teacher at a middle school in Rapid City, South Dakota. As a consultant, I was there to model student-centered coaching for a group of literacy coaches from across the district. It was the second week of school and we were feeling that sense of possibility for a new school year that you only feel in those first weeks of school.

Kristi and I had talked the week prior to begin the planning process. She shared that since it was the second week of school, she was feeling out the group and trying to reinforce the importance of reading. She clearly valued independent reading, but wanted the time to be used productively. She also wanted to make sure the students didn't get bogged down in difficult text and wanted to be aware of whether they were able to comprehend what they read.

From our first conversation, I could tell Kristi knew a lot about teaching reading. My role would be to think alongside her rather than serve as an "expert" who was coming in to tell her how to teach. In the past, I may have jumped in and began tossing ideas to Kristi. And honestly, that would have been my response as a literacy coach in years past. But my thinking about coaching has changed since then, and now I am working on being less about a set of teaching ideas and more about student learning. This shift has come from years of worry about my impact as a coach. There were too many times when I felt great about my coaching work initially—only to see little to no lasting affect on the *kids*, probably because I was focusing all my attention on the *teacher*.

As I listened to Kristi's thoughts about her instruction, I wondered how I could serve her best in the coaching session. I didn't want it to be a dog-and-pony show but instead wanted to truly add value to her work with her students. So, today it wouldn't be about my ideas. Instead it would be about designing instruction for Kristi's students. Wiggins and McTighe (2005) write,

> Deliberate and focused instructional design requires us as teachers and curriculum writers to make an important shift in our thinking about the nature of our job. The shift involves thinking a great deal, first, about the specific learnings sought, and the evidence of such learnings, before thinking about what we, as the teacher, will do or provide in teaching and learning activities. (p. 14)

With this in mind, I asked her, "What will it look like if your students successfully manage their way through difficult text?" By asking this, I shifted the conversation away from which teaching techniques Kristi could build into the lesson and toward student learning. She sat back, thought for a few minutes, and named the following goals:

1. The students will be able to recognize where they get confused.

2. The students will be able to verbalize what is confusing them.

3. The students will be able to repair their comprehension.

These goals didn't trip off Kristi's tongue, but instead were the product of thoughtful conversation and reflection. They were there when we began our conversation, but the dialogue we shared helped Kristi cull them down to a set of clear and measurable indicators of student learning. Now that we both understood her goals for the students, we could plan backward and think about the lesson. She explained, "I want to begin by defining the word metacognition as 'Paying attention to what you read so you know what you understand and what confuses you.' Then I will model how I am metacognitive when I read challenging text with *Into Thin Air* by Jon Krakauer [1997]. I think I'll stop a few times to share some strategies that I use to make sense of the text. Then I'll ask the students to do the same with a challenging excerpt from *Shipwreck at the Bottom of the World* by Jennifer Armstrong [1998]."

As I listened, I was thinking about how we could be sure we had enough concrete student evidence to guide our decision making in the debriefing session, so I asked, "What kinds of work will the students produce that we can use to guide our debriefing session?" She thought and said, "If I ask them to write notes in the margin, would that work?" I agreed that this would provide us with concrete student evidence. I also volunteered to carefully observe the students and collect more evidence while Kristi taught the lesson. That way we would have even more evidence to draw on. We both felt much more comfortable focusing on the students, and I was secretly relieved that I didn't have to have all the answers. We would let the students teach us what we needed to do next.

Collecting Student Evidence

The moment I walked into Kristi's classroom, I noticed that it didn't look like a typical middle school classroom. The overhead lights were turned off and lamps cast a soft glow. Floor-to-ceiling shelves housed a classroom library, and tables were organized in groups to allow for conversation among the students. As they arrived in class, the students immediately began reading from their self-selected chapter books. You could have heard a pin drop in the classroom full of adolescent girls and boys hunched over their books.

As Kristi prepared to teach the lesson, I took some time to reread the indicators that Kristi had shared in the planning conversation. I wanted be sure to stay focused so that the evidence we discussed in the debriefing session would be directly tied to what she was looking for. Since Kristi was building community with her students, she requested that I observe her during the lesson. This made a lot of sense and I busied myself with collecting student evidence that matched her goals for the students. Other options for the time a coach spends in the classroom include modeling instruction and co-teaching. Co-teaching is the most common for me when I'm engaged in a student-centered coaching cycle. When I'm in a teacher-centered coaching cycle, I find myself modeling instruction on a regular basis. It depends on my purpose as a coach, the relationship I have with the teacher, and the teacher's instructional knowledge and expertise. I've found that asking teachers what they are most comfortable with is the way to go.

After Kristi's modeling, I observed the students working through the text to see which of the indicators they were demonstrating. I moved around the classroom while the students were reading and recording their thinking, and I also took careful notes while they discussed their thinking during the share session. For the most part, I didn't speak much to the kids, and when I did, I asked open-ended questions like, "What did you do as a reader? What are you running into when you read this?" These open-ended questions provided me with lots of information to add to my notes and bring to the debriefing session. For a sample of my notes, see the "Tools and Techniques" section at the end of this chapter.

The bell rang for passing period, and we collected the students' work and made our way down to the conference room to see how they did. I looked forward to the conversation because not only was there substantial evidence that Kristi was already impacting the students as readers, but I imagined we would have an interesting conversation about where Kristi might go from here.

Debriefing Using Student Work

Student work (or data) is at the heart of student-centered coaching. Without student work, coaching quickly slips toward being more about teaching practice and less about student learning. Student work keeps coaching conversations grounded and specific, and propels student learning. There are many types of student work that can inform coaching conversations, and the key is deciding what would be the most relevant given the teacher's goals for the students. Examples of student work include written responses to reading, writing samples, assignments from a subject area like math or science, formal and informal assessment data, interim or benchmark assessments, anecdotal records, conferring notes, and student observation data.

After a few minutes of reflection, Kristi and I decided to dive right into the stack of student work. I suggested we sort it into three piles with similar characteristics and she agreed. We immediately noticed that a group of five students coded where they got confused and wrote down inferences to repair their understanding. They wrote things like "I'm wondering why this happened. I think it might be because . . ." These students were demonstrating exactly what Kristi had hoped for: they were thinking metacognitively and were making inferences to repair their comprehension. A much larger group of fourteen students coded several places where they were confused but didn't take the step of repairing their comprehension. With this group, we noticed that most of the notes were vocabulary-type questions such as circling words they didn't understand, writing a question mark in the margin, or writing phrases like "huh?" to indicate a lack of word knowledge. A handful of students didn't write any notes while reading. This worried Kristi. They didn't seem to be monitoring their comprehension at all and she knew this had to be established so they could continue to read and comprehend text.

After we sorted the work, I asked Kristi what she thought. She rubbed her hands through her hair and said, "I'm curious what surfaced because of my teaching. I think I need to model this again." Like so many teachers, Kristi was being way too hard on herself, so I pointed out that most of the student work showed clear evidence of some aspects of metacognition. She thought for a moment and said, "I'm happy that they were able to identify when they got confused and some even were able to repair their comprehension, but I want them to be metacognitive in more ways than just when it comes to vocabulary. And it's funny because now that I think about it, that is what I modeled in the lesson. When I did my think aloud, I really did focus on the tough vocabulary, I think because that's what the text lent itself to." This was an aha! moment for Kristi and spoke to the fact that her students were simply following her lead. In a way it gave her comfort because she knew that by providing different types of modeling, she could extend them as readers.

For Kristi, the next steps were quite clear. She now had a good sense of who needed extra support so she could more easily differentiate her instruction to the three groups that had presented themselves. She would do this by varying the texts they read and pulling some small groups. She also identified some examples from students who were demonstrating all three of the indicators and she would use these to model for the rest of the class. Finally, she planned to extend her modeling to include other ways readers get confused beyond the word level, such as at the phrase or sentence level, and this she would do with the whole class. Due to Kristi's expertise, she had no problem envisioning these next steps. But for a teacher with less background, I wouldn't have hesitated to help craft the next steps and maybe even offer to co-teach or model a few lessons alongside the teacher.

Kristi's next steps made sense and were rooted in what the students were demonstrating were their needs. I didn't have the usual coachlike worries about whether or not she would follow through because Kristi really owned these next steps. She was committed because of her desire to support her students, not to please me. As we wrapped up, I asked her if our work together was helpful and she said, "I would not have initially thought to sort the student work in this way. This process made it easier for me to look at "next steps" in my instruction. Our focus remained on student work throughout our conversation. This really helped me learn more from the student work that is in front of me every day. And now that I've done it, I hope to do more of this type of reflection on my own."

The student work helped us drill down to specific student needs in minutes. Without the student work, we would have stayed on the surface, reflecting on what Kristi did and what she could have done differently (a typical coaching conversation). Analyzing the student work allowed us to address Kristi's teaching practice because when you see something happening with your students, the natural next step is to problem-solve what to do about it. In Kristi's case, she had no trouble deciding how she would differentiate for her students and simultaneously think about how she would adapt her instruction. Herein lies the power of student-centered coaching—by focusing on students you are able to address teaching practice as well.

The Connection Between Goals for Student Learning and Teaching Practice

In a recent report in *Edutopia* (2009), Linda Darling-Hammond writes, "In the last ten years there's been a lot of research done about what makes a difference for student achievement, and it's now clear that the single most important determinant of what students learn is what their teachers know. Teacher qualifications, teacher's knowledge and skills, make more difference for student learning than any other single factor." The work of Darling-Hammond and other researchers in the area of professional development have helped create a school environment that provides high-quality support for teachers within the work day. With these structures in place, we now have the opportunity to draw upon these powerful systems for professional development and shift the lens more directly on the students. By focusing the lens on students, we can diffuse the existing pressures we feel related to "resistant" teachers since the focus isn't on improving *them* but instead is on improving the achievement of their students. Furthermore, these structures help us build a community of teachers who are skilled at analyzing student work to make decisions that best support student learning.

Several years ago, I received a request from Pam for some help. I was surprised when I received the request because, until then, Pam had been reluctant to engage in coaching even though I had approached her several times. She was a brand-new teacher who had been assigned some of the most challenging students in the fourth grade. I wanted to help, but knew that she had to be ready for it.

I began spending time in her classroom and noticed that her students were raking her over the coals on a daily basis. I realized she was suffering more than I had realized and wondered if that may have been the reason why she was hesitant to invite me in. In an attempt to get order with her students, the desks in her classroom were set up in rows, and I suggested we move them into groups so we could work together to build a more respectful community in her classroom. She halfheartedly agreed and we stayed late on a Friday afternoon rearranging desks. I would be back on Tuesday so we could start co-teaching lessons that would build community and set some expectations for her students.

When I arrived on Tuesday morning, I was shocked. The desks were back in rows and it had only been two days! I was dumbstruck. Luckily she raised the issue and confessed, "I just couldn't take it. They were talking and I couldn't get them to do their work so I moved them back last night." She made it clear that there wouldn't be any more desk moving, and as her coach I wasn't sure what to do next.

Pam is a good example of how reluctant teachers respond to teacher-centered coaching. She seemed to be on board with the coaching, but when it came time to challenge her beliefs and practices about teaching, she drew a line in the sand. Pam is the type of teacher who likes her students to be in rows, and I can't teach kids unless they are in groups. In a teacher-centered coaching model, my goal would be to get Pam to come around to my way of thinking, and if she didn't, she may even be labeled as a "resistant" teacher.

I didn't want to do that and realized that I needed a new approach. I decided to ask Pam to think about what she wanted her students to be able to do as learners. I was a little bit nervous to throw this question out there since she was a brand-new teacher. I didn't want to intimidate her, but I decided it couldn't hurt to ask. She immediately zeroed in on some work she was doing with science notebooks, "I want my kids to be able to use their science notebooks more effectively. Right now, I'm not getting much out of them."

Even though it was a little bit vague, I knew we could get more specific as we went. I figured we might as well start there rather than with me redecorating her classroom because taking this step would hopefully help us rally together around a common goal for her students.

Our first step was to figure out how her students were doing with their science notebooks. Pam was planning to do an experiment on the water cycle that week, so we decided to assess the students with the lesson she had already planned. I didn't want her to be anxious and assured her that whatever the students did with the assignment would be just fine and that I'd be there to help her figure out what to do next. She smiled and admitted, "I actually don't know what they are supposed to be able to do. I was really just focused on how to set up the experiment." This was a great opportunity to use the science standards alongside the notebooks, so we took a look at them and found three expectations for her grade level that she felt comfortable taking on. They included (1) students develop a hypothesis that is based on background knowledge, (2) students explain the steps they used to test the hypothesis, and (3) students explain how their thinking changed as a result of the experiment. To collect some assessment data, we created a simple entry for the science notebooks for the water cycle experiment.

We asked the students to do the following:

In your science notebooks explain the following:
What was your hypothesis?

How did you test your hypothesis?

In what ways did your thinking change during the experiment?

We provided very little support to students as they moved through the assignment so we could measure what they could do at an independent level. And sure enough, we noticed some clear patterns when we looked over their work. Many students were able to write a simple hypothesis like, "I think the water will evaporate." A few included background knowledge in the hypothesis, such as, "I think the water will evaporate because it is like rainwater evaporating from the street." Most of the students were even able to explain the steps they took to test the hypothesis. But where they fell short was explaining how their thinking changed as a result of the experiment. Many of the students simply restated their hypothesis, probably because they didn't have any idea what else to do.

Pam and I had a clear course. We knew that we didn't need to spend much time teaching the students how to write the steps in an experiment and that many understood how to write a hypothesis. So we decided to focus on including background knowledge as well as teaching the students to track how their thinking changes as they move through an experiment. We drew on some of the thinking strategies for reading that Pam was familiar with, and also made connections to the thinking that students were doing in math. We spent the next six weeks in an intensive coaching cycle that included the following:

- We arranged a weekly planning session to analyze student work and plan lessons.
- Once in a while I modeled lessons but we mostly co-taught lessons because I wanted to build Pam's confidence and experience level.
- After six weeks of working together, we reassessed the students by using a similar experiment and could tangibly see that they had met the goals that we had set at the beginning of our work together.

I vowed never again to mention the desk thing but about halfway through our coaching cycle, Pam brought it up. She said, "You know, I think we need to figure out a way to allow them to turn and explain their thinking in pairs so that they get used to it before they go to write it in their science notebooks. We may want to move their desks back into groups so they can do that." I smiled to myself and realized that by focusing the coaching on her students, Pam was able to move forward in her teaching practice as well. Student behavior also improved over the course of the coaching cycle due to the fact that the students became more engaged in meaningful and collaborative learning. Figure 1.2 shows the process Pam and I went through from start to finish across our six-week coaching cycle (for more on setting up coaching cycles, see Chapter 2).

Figure 1.2   Stages in a Student-Centered Coaching Cycle

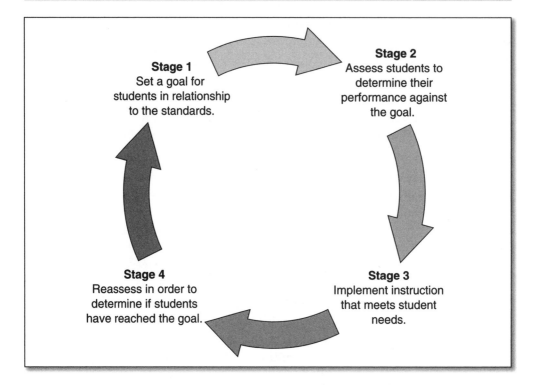

Meanwhile . . . in the Principal's Office

Many principals are concerned with a handful of struggling teachers. They know something needs to be done and a common strategy is to create a subtle (or not-so-subtle) campaign to fix these teachers. This approach can put the coach in a tricky position because at times, teachers withdraw due to feelings of apprehension, fear, and judgment. Student-centered coaching is designed to diffuse some of these fears but also hold teachers accountable for student achievement. Leading this type of coaching effort requires a specific skill set for principals that includes the following:

The Principal Understands the Purpose, Potential, and Practices for Student-Centered Coaching

Student-centered coaching requires a principal who understands the rationale and practices for this type of coaching and articulates with confidence how the coaching will positively impact students. This can be challenging because by now, many teachers have experienced some sort of teacher-centered coaching and we are working within a paradigm that has already been established. Making the shift to student-centered coaching means we have to orient (or reorient) teachers around a new vision of coaching.

Principals can benefit from studying the core components of student-centered coaching alongside their coaches. When the core practices for student-centered coaching are understood by the school leader, the leader can more readily articulate it as a valuable tool for helping teachers reach their goals for students, which, in turn, encourages teachers to fully engage in the process.

The Principal Holds Teachers Accountable for a Specific Set of Instructional Practices That Are Based on the Standards and Curriculum

It is not the coach's job to hold teachers accountable for implementing a specific curriculum or set of practices. This is the role of the school leader. Principals who support student-centered coaching put pressure on teachers and hold them accountable for practices that are based on the standards and curriculum. They view the coach as a source of support to help teachers get there.

The Principal Builds a Culture of Learning in the School

For student-centered coaching to succeed, we have to adopt a learning stance schoolwide. No longer are there "veteran" teachers who have it all figured out and "newbie" teachers who don't. No longer is the principal a manager who oversees the basic operations of the school. Instead, we are all learners in a venture to more directly address the needs of our students. Roland Barth (1995) writes, "The more crucial role of the principal is as head learner, engaging in the most important enterprise of the schoolhouse—experiencing, displaying, modeling, and celebrating what it is hoped and expected that teachers and pupils will do" (p. 80).

The Principal Navigates the Complexities of Adult Learning

Navigating the landscape of adult learning can be tricky, and the more school leaders understand about adult learners, the better position they are in to support the coaching effort. Factors such as coaching across learning styles, genders, and generation are explored in Chapter 8.

Tools and Techniques

Note-Taking Tools

How I observe teachers and take notes has changed as I've become more student centered in my coaching work. In the past, I used a two-column note-taking format where I wrote my questions and ideas on one side and a description of the lesson on the other (Figure 1.3). In the debriefing session, I shared my thinking and ideas with the teacher and assumed that he or she would run off to use the myriad of brilliant teaching strategies that I suggested. Now, when I spend time in the classroom, the lens is on the students. I focus my attention on collecting evidence about what the students do using a note-taking tool that is designed for this purpose (Figure 1.4).

Figure 1.3 Teacher-Centered Coaching Notes

Questions/Thoughts/Ideas:	Lesson:
• How many students are ELL? • I wonder what type of comprehension instruction students have had in the earlier grades? • A next step might be to have the students do this in other genres. • Some struggling readers will need extra help. • How will this happen?	• Teacher defines metacognition. • Teacher reads aloud from *Into Thin Air.* • Students are quiet and engaged. • Teacher writes her thinking in the margins of the text and talks with the students about why she was confused by the text. • Teacher hands out the excerpt from *Shipwreck at the Bottom of the World* and students begin reading and jotting notes in the margins. • Students raise hands when they need clarification. • Some students talk to one another in a productive manner. • A few students share at the end of the class period; they focus on what they did to get unstuck.

Figure 1.4   Student-Centered Coaching Notes

Indicators:

1. The students will be able to recognize where they get confused
2. The students will be able to verbalize what is confusing them
3. The students will be able to repair their comprehension

Evidence:

- When I asked, several students were able to name a place in the text that confused them, i.e., Charise, Michael, Javier, Renee (Indicator #1)
- Students worked to figure it out before moving on in their reading, i.e., Mayra, Conner, Renee (Indicators #1 and #3)
- Most students' confusion came from vocabulary words. They were able to note which words were confusing them (Indicator # 2)
- Almost all the students marked between three and five places that confused them mostly by circling unknown words, underlining a portion of the text, or writing a question mark in the margin (Indicator #1)
- A few students wrote inferences in the margin as a tool for trying to repair their comprehension, i.e., Sammy, Lexi, Thomas (Indicator #3)
- During the share session, students shared places where they got confused (Indicator #1), and some even shared how they went about thinking through ways to repair their comprehension, i.e., Madison, Charise, Christopher (Indicator #3)

Student-Centered Coaching Rubric

The following assessment is a guide to reflect on both the principal's and coach's progress toward establishing a student-centered effort. This portion is one of several traits in the rubric, and the full rubric is available in the Resources (Figure 1.5).

Figure 1.5   Student-Centered Coaching Rubric

Trait: Understands and Implements Student-Centered Coaching			
	Accomplished	*Developing*	*Novice*
The coach . . .	Student learning directly and consistently informs coaching conversations. The coach seamlessly guides the conversation from student learning to other factors, such as the implementation of a program or curriculum, and classroom routines.	The coach is beginning to draw on student data in coaching sessions. The coach is more capable in addressing other factors such as the implementation of a program or curriculum, and classroom routines in the context of student learning.	The coach rarely draws from student data in coaching sessions. Coaching is consistently focused on teaching practice, implementation of a program or curriculum, or classroom routines.

(Continued)

Figure 1.5 (Continued)

	Accomplished	Developing	Novice
The school leader . . .	The principal understands the core practices for student-centered coaching, subscribes to those practices, and provides support to move the coach's work forward.	The principal has some knowledge of the core practices for student-centered coaching or may question its value.	The principal is not supportive of, or lacks knowledge in, the core practices for student-centered coaching.
	The principal provides the necessary pressure and support to the adult learners in the school.	The principal is beginning to find a balance between providing the adequate pressure and support to the adult learners in the school.	The principal has not yet achieved a balance of providing pressure and support to the adult learners in the school.

Note: See the Resources for the full rubric.

Language for Student-Centered Coaching

Coaches often ask me for ideas about what language to use in their coaching conversations. The following questions are simple and help keep the conversation focused on student learning (DuFour, Eaker, & DuFour, 2005).

- What is it we want all students to learn?
- How will we know when each student has mastered the essential learning?
- How will we respond when a student experiences initial difficulty in learning?
- How will we deepen the learning for students who have already mastered the essential knowledge and skills? (p. 15)

Others guiding questions that I like:

- In a perfect world, describe to me what the learning would look like among your students?
- What is your goal for students in this lesson? How will that look?
- How will we collect evidence to see what they can do?
- What are our next steps based on the evidence we collected?

A Final Thought

It is my firm belief that educators are more comfortable when the conversation puts student learning front and center. When this isn't the case, we tend to feel attacked or vulnerable to the judgments and opinions of others—entering into what Jim Knight terms a "vicious cycle" of blame. He writes (2007),

> When educational leaders see their one-shot programs failing to catch fire, they start searching for reasons for that failure. Not surprisingly, teachers are often blamed for "resisting change." In turn, teachers, feeling slighted by their leaders, tell each other "this too will pass" whenever a new innovation is introduced. Ultimately, both educational leaders and teachers get caught in a vicious cycle of blame and resistance. (p. 3)

By changing the focus from fixing teachers to improving student learning, the coaching paradigm can take on new meaning for us all. And lest we forget, coaches cannot do this alone. We need our school leader to stand by our side to see the vision of school-based coaching to reality.

2

Getting Student-Centered Coaching Up and Running

I t's a late summer day as I navigate my way to an elementary school in a leafy suburb north of Chicago. Today, I'll be working with a brand-new literacy coach and thoughts are racing through my head as I anticipate how to help Mary Sue transition from veteran teacher to literacy coach.

Like most coaches, Mary Sue comes from the teaching ranks, where the day is structured by ringing bells, recess schedules, and a specific amount of minutes designated for each subject area. Coaching is different. Coaches are given a blank slate to shape how they will spend their time for the greatest impact. My goal for the day is to help Mary Sue do just that.

Mary Sue is not alone in her shift to becoming a coach. In fact, we have all been engaged in a significant shift over the past two decades as we strive to find a model for teacher learning that gets results with students. In his seminal book, *The Predictable Failure of Educational Reform,* Seymour Sarason (1990) writes, "It is virtually impossible to create and sustain over time conditions for productive learning for students when they do not exist for teachers" (p. 145). Sarason's work makes the case for the coherent and well-designed professional development that Mary Sue will provide to her colleagues.

Coaching in the First Few Weeks of School

As a teacher, I loved the hot days in late July when I'd return to school to set up my classroom. The book bins would be just so. The desks set up in groups. The daily schedule carefully penned next to the board. Fresh off of summer professional development sessions and lots of reading, I felt renewed and was excited to be teaching again.

When I became a literacy coach, I wasn't sure how to most productively spend my time in the first few weeks of school. Instead of setting up my own classroom, I wandered around the school offering my services, "Would you like help moving desks?" "Need help organizing book bins?" The hardest part was the first day of school, when I stood to the side as the teachers carried their lists out to the blacktop to meet their classes. Children with brand-new school clothes and backpacks were lined up and ready to love their new teacher. Hugs were shared, welcomes given, and off they marched into their classrooms. There I stood. It was too early to start "coaching" and I couldn't hang out in the front office or everybody would know that I didn't have anything to do.

James Flaherty (1999) emphasizes the importance of establishing relationships in the early stages of coaching. He writes, "Relationship remains the beginning point of coaching and its foundation. I keep bringing it up because this is the stage that more than any other is neglected, ignored, or considered to be unnecessary. Given that it's the foundation, it can cause the most problems when it is taken for granted. The basic ingredients for the relationship are mutual trust, respect, and freedom of expression" (p. 39).

With this in mind, it was clear that I had a lot of work to do to build mutual trust, respect, and freedom of expression with teachers in these early weeks of school. But I didn't want that to be my only goal. It was also important for the coaching to increase student achievement. These felt like competing forces . . . just focusing on relationships seemed to be too touchy feely and holding teachers accountable for student learning seemed heavy handed. I wasn't sure which way to go.

Now I've found a middle ground between these polarities. I don't look at it as if I am holding teachers accountable for increasing student achievement. Instead, my role is to help teachers reach their goals for students. Though seemingly subtle, this has been a significant shift in how I view my role as a coach. Now, in the first few days and weeks of school, I focus on the following tasks:

- Calibrate how I view my coaching role with the principal
- Define student-centered coaching for teachers and call for their participation

- Set the coaching focus with teachers who are ready to go
- Build a schedule that makes an impact with students and teachers
- Monitor and develop my relationships with all teachers

No more wandering around the school during those first few weeks. There is important work to do to frame the coaching model and get teachers involved. Here's more on how that looks.

Calibrate My Coaching Role With the Principal

Defining how you see yourself as a coach is an important first step. More often than not, coaches take this process lightly, assuming that once they get started, their role will define itself. Or coaches forget to calibrate what they perceive to be their role with the principal, which creates a confusing environment of mixed messages for teachers.

Mary Sue and her principal started the year by planning how they would unveil coaching to the teachers. Since she was transitioning from teacher to coach in the same school, it was vital for Mary Sue to carefully communicate her new role to her peers. As her principal, Neal wanted to get the word out to teachers through a carefully crafted coaching model that took into account their separate, but complementary, roles. He described his vision for how to organize the professional development and what he saw as Mary Sue's role within that structure:

- Whole-Group Professional Development. Mary Sue would take the lead on whole-group sessions focusing on literacy. She and Neal would plan the sessions based on what they were seeing in the student data as well as on the expectations of their district.
- Small-Group Professional Development. Mary Sue would facilitate a kindergarten Professional Learning Community (PLC) every few weeks. She would provide targeted support for the teachers who work with English-language learners (ELL), and lead monthly meetings for the new teachers on staff.
- One-on-One Coaching. Mary Sue would provide intensive coaching support on an opt-in basis. Her coaching would link to the other work she was doing with teachers and would be based on goals for student learning.

Peter Senge has been guiding us through leadership and organizational change for two decades. He writes, "It is becoming clear that schools can be re-created, made vital, and sustainably renewed not by fiat or command, and not by regulation, but by taking a *learning orientation"* (2000, p. 5). Neal would take a cue from this by creating a fine balance of pressure and support so that student and teacher learning would move forward. He would honor the role that he and Mary Sue had defined by encouraging teachers to participate in the coaching. And he would hold teachers accountable by setting the tone that "we are all learners here."

Define Student-Centered Coaching for Teachers and Call for Their Participation

While it is essential to define what student-centered coaching means for the teachers and students, it can be equally important to define what coaching isn't so that myths are debunked and teachers can move past the traditional coaching paradigm. This is an opportunity to build buzz and excitement about coaching so teachers see how it will positively affect their students.

Neal and Mary Sue started by introducing the new coaching model to each and every teacher at a faculty meeting. Mary Sue defined how she saw her work evolving and Neal made sure there was no question as to whether he supported and trusted Mary Sue in her coaching role.

After the full faculty had been informed, Mary Sue shared her plans for how she would organize her time as a coach. In order to be clear and well understood, she wrote a welcome letter and polled teachers to gauge their interest. Her materials carefully reinforced how she viewed her role while encouraging teachers to get involved in a way that made sense to them. See "Tools and Techniques" at the end of this chapter for Mary Sue's welcome letter.

As a result of her careful planning and communication, eighteen teachers indicated an interest in participating in one-on-one coaching with Mary Sue. Their ideas about what to work on varied, and included things like the following:

- Setting up guided reading groups
- Teaching spelling and word study
- Using running records
- Teaching the comprehension strategies
- Teaching writer's workshop
- Nonfiction reading strategies
- Leveling guided reading books

She was relieved to know that so many teachers viewed her as a valuable source of support, but now she had to figure out how to best meet the teachers' varying needs. Their interests included the usual combination of teacher-centered topics like leveling guided reading books, using running records, and setting up guided reading groups. But there were also a few student-centered topics, including nonfiction reading strategies, spelling, word study, and reading comprehension. Most of the topics were broad and needed some narrowing down, but they were on the right track.

Set the Coaching Focus With Teachers Who Are Ready to Go

During today's visit, Mary Sue had scheduled preliminary conversations with several of the teachers who had indicated an interest in working with her. She had a basic sense of what they wanted help with, and I would help guide the conversation to focus directly on something the teachers wanted the students to learn. Once we had that figured out, we could create a schedule that would meet everyone's needs.

Many times, teachers request a teacher-centered focus for coaching. In these cases, it is up to the coach to help the teacher take a step back to discover their goals for students. The following conversation is an example of how I help teachers shift the focus toward a more explicit goal for students (Figures 2.1 and 2.2).

Figure 2.1   Sample Coaching Conversation: Focusing a Coaching Cycle on Student Learning (Elementary)

Coach:	I noticed on your survey that you are looking for help setting up guided reading groups. Can you tell me a bit more about this?
Teacher:	I came from a different district and we used a strict reading program. I know I'm supposed to be doing guided reading groups, but I'm not sure how. I have all of these books to use, but to be honest, they haven't left the boxes because I'm really not sure what to do with them.
Coach:	Let's talk a little bit about your students. How would you describe them as readers?
Teacher:	They are across the board, like most second graders. Some are reading and others are barely able to recognize common sight words. It's overwhelming.
Coach:	What are your hopes for your students as readers? What do you want them to master by the end of the year?

(Continued)

Figure 2.1 (Continued)

Teacher:	I'd really like to see them comprehending whatever they read, no matter what level reader they are. I know that inferring is an important standard, and that is a goal I have for my students.
Coach:	That makes a lot of sense. How would you feel about focusing on inferring, and we can do that in the context of guided reading? That way we can work together to set up guided reading groups and dive into your materials, all with a goal in mind that you have for your students. We can even do some pre- and postassessing to see if we are on the right track.
Teacher:	I love that idea because it feels doable but also as though we are taking on something that I'm supposed to be doing.
Coach:	Terrific! Our next step will be to figure out how we will preassess your students to see how they are doing with inferring, and then we can plan instruction that will incorporate guided reading. Why don't we meet at the same time next week?
Teacher:	Thanks!

Figure 2.2　Sample Coaching Conversation: Focusing a Coaching Cycle on Student Learning (Middle School)

Coach:	I see that you would like to participate in a coaching cycle. What do you have in mind?
Teacher:	To be honest, it's my third-hour algebra class. The kids' behavior is really challenging. I thought you might have some classroom management ideas that could help.
Coach:	Let's talk a little bit about that course. What are you working on now in terms of mathematical skills?
Teacher:	We are focusing on order of operations. But that's really not what I need help with since I'm following the district math program, and the rest of my classes are doing fine and learning the material. I need help with classroom management.
Coach:	Okay, I hear you on that. What sort of positive behaviors in your other classes would you like to see in the third hour?
Teacher:	We do a lot of sharing of thinking on the SMART Board, and I'd like to see the kids listening to one another and asking questions to clarify their own thinking. I'd like to see them treating each other with more respect. And, I'd like to be sure that they take responsibility to learn the material.
Coach:	It sounds like a big goal for this class would be being learners that are accountable for their own learning as well as the learning of others.
Teacher:	Yeah, I guess so.
Coach:	How about if we focus on those behaviors with the class? The ideas you listed were a great start on a rubric we could design, maybe even with the kids, that would be how we would assess their progress. Then at the end of our coaching cycle, we can see how they've progressed in demonstrating these behaviors.
Teacher:	I think it would really help to work with you on this. It sounds like we may come up with some good ideas.
Coach:	I agree. We'll get started when we meet in a few days.

What teachers bring as topics for coaching varies greatly. Elementary teachers typically focus on teaching programs or practices that they would like to implement in their classroom. Middle school teachers are more often interested in issues around student engagement, classroom management, and sometimes on specific teaching practices. I often advise coaches at this level to view student behaviors as rich topics for student-centered coaching. Of course this differs from teacher to teacher, school to school, district to district, and it is up to the coach to design a conversation that uncovers the teachers' goals for students.

Coaching Cycles

Effective professional development provides continued follow-up, support, and pressure that can only be delivered by a school-based coach. Thomas Guskey (1995) writes, "Fitting new practices and techniques to unique on-the-job conditions is an uneven process that requires extra time and extra effort, especially when beginning. Guidance, direction, and support with pressure are crucial when these adaptations are being made" (p. 123).

One way to provide the necessary support is by organizing coaching into cycles in which coaches create a structure for their time that allows for sustained collaboration over a period of time. Coaching cycles have the following characteristics:

- They involve in-depth work with a teacher or pair of teachers, lasting approximately six to nine weeks.
- They focus on something that comes from either formal or informal student data.
- They include regular planning sessions, such as a 30- to 50-minute planning session per week and one to three times per week in the classroom for co-teaching, modeling instruction, or observing the teaching and learning.

Coaching cycles are a portion of a coach's overall work. Other duties may include planning and facilitating small- and large-group professional development, managing data and assessment, gathering resources, mentoring, having informal planning sessions, and helping teachers organize their materials. With such a broad range of duties, a typical coach can take on four to six coaching cycles at a time and less if the coach works less than full-time. Every teacher really doesn't need to be coached throughout the school year, and it is realistic for each teacher in a school to participate in one or two cycles over the course of the year. That isn't to say that they aren't engaged in professional development when they aren't in a coaching cycle. In most schools, teachers are expected to participate in other forms of professional development, such as full faculty professional development sessions, grade-level or department meetings, professional learning communities, informal coaching support, and other voluntary learning opportunities.

Building a Schedule That Impacts Students and Teachers

Creating a schedule that has the potential to most greatly impact student learning sometimes feels like the first hurdle for a coach. Coaches often worry about overstepping and expecting too much from teachers. This, they fear, may damage budding relationships. The result can be an awkward situation akin to a first date. The teacher is thinking, "Sure, I'll go along. It sounds like a good idea. I hope the coach approves of what I'm doing in my classroom." The coach is thinking, "I really hope the teacher finds this time with me to be meaningful. I hope I'll be invited back for more." Many coaches make apologies for asking teachers to work with them. It seems that they feel as if they are taking up the teachers' valuable planning time. I encourage coaches to view their support as a commodity rather than a burden, especially since the focus is on making a clear and measurable impact on the students.

It is true that time is a limited resource for teachers and we have to be somewhat flexible and sensitive to this reality. With that in mind, the first step is to reach a set of agreements about what both the teacher and coach are expecting. Rather than beating around the bush, I get right to the point with the following questions so I am sure I know what the teacher is hoping to get out of the relationship as well as what the teacher is willing to invest in terms of time and reflection (Figure 2.3).

Figure 2.3   Teacher and Coach Agreement

1. What do you hope students will learn as a result of our coaching work?
2. Is there any student work or data that could help us decide on a focus that would make the most impact with students?
3. How would you like to interact during our time in the classroom (co-teach, model, observe)?
4. I suggest a weekly planning session for 30 to 45 minutes; what time works for you?
5. It is also important for me to be in your classroom for one to three times per week; what time is best for you based on your goal for students?
6. How would you like to communicate between our planning sessions? (meetings, e-mails, other)
7. Do you have any other concerns about the coaching?
8. Is there anything you want me to be sure to do as your coach?

Once a shared set of expectations has been established, coaches have the information they need to develop a schedule that takes this information into account. The following coaching schedule (Figure 2.4) comes from my work at an elementary school that was establishing independent reading schoolwide (See "Tools and Techniques" later in this chapter for a middle school coaching schedule).

For being so early in the year, it is a good mix between student- and teacher-centered coaching. Though the goal is to be as student centered as possible, I would never turn away a teacher

Figure 2.4 Elementary Coaching Schedule

First Coaching Cycle—August–October					
	Monday	*Tuesday*	*Wednesday*	*Thursday*	*Friday*
9:00–9:50	Sandra (3rd): Students will choose just right books	Jeff (2nd): Students understand differences between narrative and informational texts	Sandra (3rd): Students will choose just right books	Jeff (2nd): Students understand differences between narrative and informational texts	Plan with Danielle
10:00–10:50	First-grade team meeting	Geni (1st): Students will choose just right books	Geni (1st): Students will choose just right books	Geni (1st): Students will choose just right books	Plan with Susan
11:00–11:50	Second-grade team meeting	Danielle (1st): Students build stamina during independent reading	Susan (5th): Helping students manage the classroom library	Danielle (1st): Students build stamina during independent reading	Susan (5th): Helping students manage the classroom library
12:00–12:30	Third-grade team meeting	Lunch	Lunch	Lunch	Lunch
12:30–1:00	Fourth-grade team meeting	Informal planning with teachers	Informal planning with teachers	Informal planning with teachers	Informal planning with teachers
1:00–1:50	Fifth-grade team meeting	Joanna (K): Reading conferences	Joanna (K): Reading conferences	Joanna (K): Reading conferences	Plan with Jeff
2:00–2:50	ECE/Kinder team meeting	Meet with the principal	Plan with Maria	Plan with Joanna	Plan with Sandra and Geni
3:00–3:50	My planning	My planning	My planning	My planning	My planning

who honestly needed help with something based in classroom management or on teaching practice. Examples of student-centered coaching foci are these:

- Sandra and Geni chose to team to figure out how to teach their students to choose just right books.
- Jeff is starting the year with work on the characteristics of different genres so he wanted help with that.
- Danielle's students need help building stamina as younger readers.

Others are geared toward helping teachers with questions about their practice:

- Susan has struggled with the organization of her classroom library and wanted to figure out some organizational strategies to make her classroom run smoother.
- Joanna is a newer teacher trying to learn how to confer with students about their independent reading.

A few other things you may notice about the schedule:

1. As a full-time coach, the most coaching cycles I can manage at one time are with four to six teachers. If I was a part-time coach or if I had other duties, that number would decrease.

2. Small-group learning, like grade-level meetings and one-on-one coaching, are balanced across the week and are a big part of my responsibilities.

3. A meeting with the principal takes place on a weekly basis.

4. Teachers like Sandra and Geni can be paired up in planning sessions if they are focused on the same topic and are comfortable collaborating.

5. As a coach, I have the same amount of planning time as the teachers.

6. I allow some flexible time for informal coaching and planning with teachers so that when someone needs something, I can get it to them quickly. My choice for this time is when students are at lunch because that's the time teachers like to drop in to see me.

Other Things to Consider When Scheduling

- *Make your schedule public.* Teachers often wonder how a coach spends his or her time. Sometimes they are even suspicious of the flexibility that a coach has throughout the day. Rather than breed suspicion, I suggest coaches display their schedule in a public place and send it out regularly to teachers. If for some reason the coach is gone for a meeting or training, it is important for teachers to be updated regarding when and why the coach will be out of the building. Sometimes coaches are uncomfortable listing names of teachers on their schedule in a public manner. They worry that the teachers may feel that being on the coach's schedule makes them look as if they aren't performing in their job. My feeling is if the school has defined coaching as student centered, than this becomes a non-issue. After all, don't we all have goals about student learning? If the coaching model is more geared toward improving struggling teachers, than this may indeed be something to consider. This is one that I leave up to the coach to decide.

- *Update the schedule every few months.* Since a full-time coach can only manage four to six coaching cycles at a time, it is important to reengage teachers on a regular basis. That way, if a teacher missed out on the first round, he or she can be accommodated later. Coaches sometimes struggle with asking teachers to wait, so they squeeze too many onto their schedule, but just like with good teaching it is better to go deep than shallow.

- *Spend one to three days a week in the classroom and plan weekly with teachers.* The heart of the coaching takes place during planning sessions with teachers. Time in the classroom is about collecting evidence of student learning, supporting the teacher in some of the teaching responsibilities, and having a deep understanding of the classroom context. Sending the message that you need to be in the classroom every day sends the message that you don't have full confidence in the teacher's abilities. Trust the teacher and invest your time in meaningful planning sessions.

Developing Relationships With All Teachers

Now that I have a sense of the teachers who are on board and ready to engage in the coaching, I need to reflect on the rest of the staff. Just like in a classroom of students, there are teachers who blend into the background and it is up to me to work toward engaging them in the coaching. Just as I used to do with my students, I find it important to monitor the development of relationships so that I can be sure nobody falls through the cracks. Rather than trying to keep it all in my head, I use the following tool (Figure 2.5) to keep track of how my relationships are progressing, what I'm learning about teachers, and possible openings for coaching. I do this with each and every teacher so I can monitor those that I haven't connected with. Sometimes I am surprised by what I learn about people when I sit down to talk with them. Sometimes I am surprised by my own reticence to take the step to learn about my colleagues. And sometimes I am surprised by how little I might know about the people who are right down the hall.

Figure 2.5 Monitoring Relationships

Teacher Name	Skills/Interests/Goals	Status of the Coaching	Possible Coaching Openings
Ofelia	• Strong background in English language acquisition • Native Spanish speaker • New mom	• May participate in a coaching cycle later in the year	• Blending social studies content into book clubs • She has shown an interest in learning more about reading comprehension
Mark	• Passionate about letting students be themselves • Background in constructivist teaching • Sings in a choir on the weekends	• Said he would participate in a coaching cycle but he doesn't seem totally on board	• Feels limited by the district literacy program • Wants to figure out how to keep doing what he has been doing but knows that he will have to adjust a little bit

Meanwhile . . . in the Principal's Office

Principals often ask how to encourage reluctant teachers to participate in coaching. They feel that the opportunity shouldn't only be for teachers who are willing, interested, and reflective. But they also know that if they assign teachers to work with a coach, then this may jeopardize the trust that the coach is building with teachers. It can feel like a slippery slope for principals who want to support the coaching and also see results. Principals can help get the coaching up and running by using these strategies:

Being in Classrooms

With a principal's workload, it can be tempting to spend less time in classrooms when there is a coach on staff. Principals may feel that the coach knows more about instructional practice than they do. Or perhaps the principal is bogged down in other issues. It sounds counterintuitive, but when there is a coach on staff, it is essential for the principal to spend time in classrooms. Short visits are just fine, because it is about the principal's visibility and personal knowledge of what is happening out in classrooms that matters. Boston principal Kim Marshall writes, "Short, unannounced classroom visits are the best way for principals to see representative slices of teaching (not the dog-and-pony show), give credible feedback to teachers, and be players in improving teaching and learning" (*Education Week*, pp. 24–25). Without this personal knowledge and contact, teachers will become distrustful and worry that the coach is reporting their flaws back to the principal.

Providing Teachers With Options for Participation

When designing a professional development model that provides many ways for teachers to engage in professional development, some aspects of professional development may be optional, such as coaching or study groups, while others aren't, such as grade-level or department meetings. By having a tiered system with a variety of options, teachers can engage and feel comfortable, and the coach can work toward building a trusting relationship that can take them further.

Determining a Schoolwide Focus for Teacher and Student Learning

One of the first items on a coach's wish list is to have a clear focus for teacher learning that has been articulated by the principal. With a clear focus, the coach can engage teachers in something that they perceive is expected and meaningful. It also helps the coach manage the workload and makes it easier for the coach to make connections across one-on-one coaching, small-group learning, and large-group professional development sessions.

After the focus for the coaching has been determined, the principal and coach can make a plan for how they will assess student learning across time. Some schools have plenty of assessments to draw on for this purpose, while others may have to develop some intermediary assessments to measure student learning.

Committing to Weekly or Biweekly Meetings With the Coach

The coach depends on a regular time to check in, plan, and problem-solve with the principal. Without this time, the coach quickly begins to feel very alone. For more on what to talk about during these meetings, see Chapter 7.

Tools and Techniques

Principal/Coach Agreement

The Principal/Coach Agreement (Figure 2.6) is a tool for the principal and coach to calibrate the coaching role. It leads the principal and coach through a discussion of important decisions about the focus of professional development, their respective roles in enacting professional development, and agreements about principal and coach communication. Rather than making assumptions about these important issues, the principal and coach craft a partnership right from the start.

Figure 2.6   Principal/Coach Agreement

I. THE WORK

On what topics/areas should we focus to improve student learning?

- How has or might student data inform this decision?
- If necessary, how will we gather the appropriate student data? (student work samples, tests, etc.)
- How will we collect data across time to demonstrate the impact of coaching on teacher and student learning?

II. DEFINING OUR ROLES

- What roles and responsibilities will we each have in leading professional development? (large group, small group, and one-on-one)

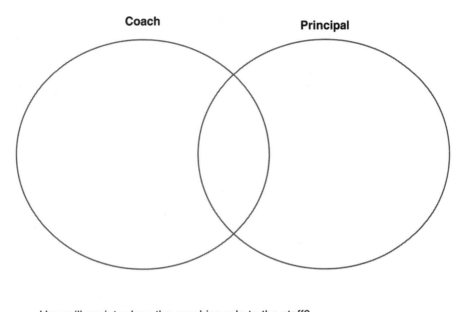

Coach   **Principal**

- How will we introduce the coaching role to the staff?

III. ONGOING COMMUNICATION AND SCHEDULING

- How and when will we communicate?
- What will the coach's schedule look like?
- How will we support each other?

Welcome Letter

Mary Sue's welcome letter and teacher survey (Figure 2.7) expressed her hopes for her new role as a coach while also laying some ground work for what she expected from teachers. Erring on the side of more communication and clarity is always the best way to go.

Middle School Coaching Schedule

Coaching schedules in the older grades often include a slightly different set of roles and responsibilities. In contrast to elementary coaches, many middle school coaches teach at least one instructional block and then fill in the rest of their time with coaching duties. The schedule shown in Figure 2.8 comes from a middle school instructional coach, and includes an instructional block as well as small-group and one-on-one coaching.

Figure 2.7   Welcome Letter and Interest Survey

Dear Teachers:

I am so eager to begin working together. My main purpose as a literacy coach is to support and assist staff members to reach their goals for student learning. I look forward to partnering with you to reach your goals for students. In addition to working alongside you in a small-group setting, I would like the opportunity to work with you in a formal coaching cycle that will last approximately six to nine weeks. I am also available for informal planning support if you are interested. These will be one-time planning sessions and will have less impact on your students' achievement due to their informal nature.

In a formal coaching cycle, we will work together to look at student work, plan lessons, and co-teach. You will choose the focus based on what would benefit your students the most. Once a week we will meet together for a 30- to 45-minute planning session to analyze assessments or student work, discuss lessons and teaching methods, and use this information to drive further instruction.

I hope to get the opportunity to work with you and your students. Please keep in mind that my calendar fills on a first-come, first-served basis, so please complete and return the attached interest survey as soon as possible. Also remember that my schedule will change each quarter so that I can accommodate everyone's needs. If you would like to participate at a later date, just let me know.

Thank you for giving this your thoughtful consideration. I look forward to working with you.

Sincerely,

Mary Sue

Name:_____

_____ I would like to participate in a coaching cycle

_____ I would like to set up an informal coaching session

1. What would you like to focus on?
   _____

2. What are your goals for your students?
   _____

3. What is the best time to set up a weekly planning session?
   _____

4. Based on your goals for students, what is the best time for me to work with you in your classroom?
   _____

Figure 2.8 Middle School Coaching Schedule

Coaching Schedule—September 1–October 31					
	Monday	*Tuesday*	*Wednesday*	*Thursday*	*Friday*
7:30–8:00	Advisory With 8th Graders				
8:00–9:00	Teach Pre-Algebra				
9:10–10:10	Training with other coaches from the district	Tom (Pre-Calculus): Students learn to solve inverse functions	Sally (Lang Arts): Students will use accountable talk in book discussions	Tom (Pre-Calculus): Students learn to solve inverse functions	Sally (Lang Arts): Students will use accountable talk in book discussions
10:20–11:30		Prep for coaching	Lunch	Prep for coaching	Meeting with special education/ ELL team
11:30–12:00	Lunch	Lunch	Meet with Data Team	Lunch	Lunch
12:10–1:00	Planning with the Lang Arts Team	John (Biology): Student engagement and classroom management during labs	Planning with the Math Team	John (Biology): Student engagement and classroom management during labs	Planning with the Science Team
1:10–2:00	Plan with Sally	Informal planning with teachers	Plan with John	Meeting with the principal and assistant principal	Informal planning with teachers
2:10–3:00	Prep for pre-coaching	Prep for Pre-Algebra	Prep for Pre-Algebra	Prep for Pre-Algebra	Prep for pre-coaching
3:00–3:30	After-school tutoring	Meeting with new teachers for mentoring	After-school tutoring	Informal planning with teachers	Plan with Tom

A Final Thought

Getting coaching up and running can be both exhilarating and terrifying. Coaches are excited to be doing such important work, but many struggle to create systems for their work that are both manageable and get results. The tools and strategies in this chapter have been designed to provide structure along with a degree of flexibility. Using them without considering the school's goals, student data, and culture may backfire. Therefore, it is necessary for the principal and coach to use these materials in a way that builds on what exists and takes the learning forward.

Wandering around a school without direction is never a good feeling. When a principal and coach work together to craft a system for coaching, it becomes a sustainable enterprise that everyone in the school can engage in and benefit from.

3

Crafting a Culture of Learning

One of the toughest aspects of improving schools is managing through issues of climate and culture. We often focus on creating systems and structures, overlook the underlying culture, and are then surprised when things fall apart. More than once, I have found myself at a barbeque and a friend with school-age kids asks, "What is the one thing that you think makes the biggest difference for schools to be successful?" My answer is inevitably, "It takes a principal who understands how to craft the school culture while simultaneously providing the necessary support for students and teachers." They nod their head, take a sip of their drink, and change the subject.

All organizations operate within a given culture. This became startlingly clear the first time I visited an Apple Store for technical support. I felt rather dowdy when I looked around and pretty much everyone in the store (employees and customers) looked as though they belonged either in an alternative rock band or posing in a fashion magazine. Techno music pumped through the store and there was a youthful and cutting-edge vibe. Do you suppose the Apple culture is an accident? Not a chance. It has been carefully designed and cultivated and has been pivotal to the company's success.

The culture in schools is also a key ingredient for success, and we could stand to learn a lot from organizations like Apple as we repeatedly underestimate our role in crafting the culture in which we operate. According to Robert Evans (1996), "A careful look at the true nature of culture and functions of organizational culture reveals that it operates at a profound level, exerting a potent influence over beliefs and behavior to preserve continuity and oppose change" (p. 41). Edgar Schein goes on to define culture as "the deeper level of *basic assumptions* and *beliefs* that are shared by members of an organization, that operate unconsciously, and that define in a basic 'taken-for-granted' fashion an organization's view of itself and its environment [italics in original]" (pg. 41). To demonstrate the challenges and possibilities related to school culture, this chapter will share concrete examples of steps that schools have taken to shape the community members' basic assumptions and beliefs to craft a culture of learning for both students and teachers.

Designing a Learning Culture

Roland Barth (2007) writes, "Probably the most important—and the most difficult—job of the school-based reformer is to change the prevailing culture of a school. The school's culture dictates, in no uncertain terms, 'the way we do things around here'" (p. 159). He goes on to say,

> And all school cultures are incredibly resistant to change. This is precisely why school improvement—from within or from without—is usually so futile. Yet unless all teachers and administrators act to change the culture of a school, all "innovations" will have to fit in and around existing elements of the culture. That is, they will be superficial window dressing, incapable of making much of a difference. (p. 160)

We can act to change our climate and culture even though it may feel fixed and entrenched. Recently I worked on a project providing support to twelve math and literacy coaches from across four schools that served mostly Spanish-speaking and low-income students. I learned valuable lessons about the role of culture as I worked alongside the coaches, teachers, and principals in each of these schools. Although in the same neighborhood, it seemed as if they were on different planets. Each school was expected to implement the same curriculum and use the same instructional practices, yet they had an entirely different tone. One day in late November, while visiting each of the schools during a districtwide professional development day, it dawned on me that the schools had taken on the personalities of their principals. This spoke volumes for how much influence school leaders really do have on school culture.

Four Studies in Culture

A Study in Culture With Karen—The Congenial School

Karen is a warm, motherly type who has raised her own children and is close to retirement. The school exudes a warm and caring atmosphere and, for today's meeting, she decorated the tables with snowflakes and teabags to celebrate the new season. When the teachers filed into the room, they were smiling and chatting. Today was the first time they had been asked to bring student work to share with their colleagues and I wondered how it would go given their congenial nature. Once their conversations got underway, I noticed that many of the teachers were pointing out what they thought was nice about the student work and weren't addressing the larger issues around student performance. Everybody left feeling pretty good about things, but that wasn't the intent of the meeting. The intent was to name some areas where students could stand to improve, and that wasn't necessarily accomplished.

Afterward, I met with the coaches and Karen and we agreed that if we wanted to help teachers go deeper in their conversations about student work, then we had to help them learn how to have collegial conversations while still honoring their congenial nature. Our next steps for crafting the school culture were the following:

- Define collegiality with teachers and discuss why developing a collegial school culture benefits students.
- Set goals with teachers for creating a school culture that is both congenial and collegial.
- Be explicit about developing the teachers' skills in discussing student work. We used the Seven Norms for Collaborative Work to help teachers set goals and reflect on their progress when engaged in these types of conversations (see "Tools and Techniques" at the end of this chapter).
- Work with the coaches to design tools and protocols for guiding conversations toward addressing the needs of the students.

A Study in Culture With Mark—The Resistant School

Mark recently replaced a long-adored principal who retired. He is a brand-new principal and since he is new to the district, he has had little experience with the district curriculum. His school has a more reserved tone that was demonstrated when the teachers filed into the meeting carrying armfuls of binders and saying very little. What a stark contrast to the smiles and teabags! The coaches had designed a session in which the teachers were asked to read and discuss a short article. I joined one of the tables and was struck by how little the teachers engaged in the conversation . . . it felt a little bit more like pulling teeth in the dentist's office than a compelling conversation. Most of the teachers sat through the meeting, nodded their heads, and then went right back to the way they had done things all along.

When we debriefed the meeting, Mark started off the conversation by saying, "Well, there clearly are some issues here. We need to figure out how to engage these teachers." Clearly the teachers felt that very little of the district curriculum applied to them and they had no intention of implementing it . . . something that was unacceptable given the fact that this was a school that had scored unsatisfactorily on the state report card for the past two years. The coaches agreed that they had run into numerous roadblocks when they tried to get the teachers to engage in the coaching and were finding that they had the same repeat customers but hadn't had much contact with a good portion of the teaching staff. Mark said, "I think some of this has to do with my lack of experience with the district curriculum, and because of that I haven't sent the message that the teachers have to do this with their kids." In order to move forward in crafting the school culture,

- Mark committed to working with his coaches to learn more about the district curriculum so he could recognize and reinforce what was expected.
- Mark and the coaches worked with the district to craft a set of instructional indicators so they could be better aligned with the district curriculum and also hold teachers accountable.
- Mark and the coaches used the indicators in conversations with teachers and sent explicit messages that these instructional methods were expected in each and every classroom.
- The school was filled with materials that dated back to the 1960s, such as outdated math books, basal readers, and stacks of reproduced worksheets. Though these materials were no longer appropriate to be used during the school day, they did have value in the community since most families had very few books or materials in the home. Mark set up a community "garage sale" in which he donated these materials to the neighborhood, ensuring that they would no longer be used in the classrooms.
- Mark and the coaches worked to replace the outdated materials with new materials that better aligned with the curriculum.
- Mark prepared himself to weather a fair amount of fallout, anger, and resentment among some of the teachers. But he

braced himself and made every effort to convey two parallel messages: "This is serious and it is the direction we will be taking" and "I will support you through this transition." This was something he was willing to endure so that he could shift the culture in the right direction.

A Study in Culture With Maria—The Overwhelmed School

Maria led the largest school in the district, with over 800 students from low-income homes. She believed wholeheartedly in the district curriculum and was very comfortable setting expectations for teachers to implement it in their classrooms. Due to its size and number of Title I students, the school had two literacy coaches and a math coach. Maria saw it as her duty to be involved in every classroom, a tall order in such a large school. She was pulled in many directions and worked long hours right alongside the teachers, many of whom were new to the profession and needed lots of support. This made them more open to the coaching but also easily overwhelmed.

Today's meeting was shaping up to be jam-packed. The district was in the middle of purchasing classroom libraries for every school and the coaches wanted to get the teachers' feedback about what to purchase. There was an article to read and discuss about teaching English-language learners, and a teacher was planning to share some ideas she was using for teaching math. It is pretty easy to predict what happened. The conversation about materials took longer than expected, which squeezed short the article discussion, and then left the teacher presenting to a group of teachers who were anxious about getting back to their classrooms. Not ideal.

After the meeting, the coaches and Maria were exhausted. They each felt frantic and frazzled and it occurred to them that the teachers must be feeling the same way. They needed to get focused or nobody would survive the school year. Their next steps for crafting the school culture were the following:

- Set some priorities using their midyear assessment data. They decided to set two goals for student learning, one for literacy and one for math, and then focus on those goals for a few months so they could slow down the pace for teachers.
- They would find ways to measure their progress and when they felt that these objectives were accomplished, they would move on to a new set of goals.

- The coaches committed to taking a less-is-more approach in order to create quality conversations among the staff. They would plan meetings together so they could manage the flow and content of the sessions.

A Study in Culture With Marsha—The Laid-Back School

Marsha has a hilarious sense of humor and a dynamic personality, and is what you would call a "people person." The tone in her school is lighthearted and laid-back despite the fact that it serves over 98% of students on free and reduced lunch and is located in a neighborhood rife with gang violence. The teachers do quite a bit of socializing outside of school and know each other as both coworkers and friends.

Today the teachers would be meeting in small groups based on their choice of topics that include conferring with students in all subject areas, using the workshop model in math, and using small-group instruction to support struggling learners. Given the friendly and relaxed culture in Marsha's school, I wondered how the teachers would work together. The two coaches had designed the sessions thoughtfully, and I hoped that the teachers would dig into the more complex issues surrounding their students and their learning. As I listened to the groups, I noticed that the conversations were guided by the Consultancy Protocol (see "Tools and Techniques" at the end of this chapter) and that the protocol was helping to keep the discussions focused. I knew we were on the right track when I overheard a teacher comment, "This meeting was really valuable. It felt different from our usual grade-level meetings."

As we debriefed the meeting, the role of the protocol came up right away. Marsha said, "I really didn't think a protocol was necessary and I thought it may turn off some teachers. But I think it really helped keep us on track." The coaches agreed and shared that they thought this meeting had a very different feel from previous ones where teachers took their time together as an opportunity for socializing rather than tackling the complex issues they faced as teachers. They decided that their next steps for crafting the school culture were these:

- The coaches would provide more structure when leading large- and small-group sessions.
- Marsha agreed to support the use of protocols even though they didn't necessarily match her learning style.
- The coaches would work with the teachers to set goals for student learning in their grade-level teams to add further focus to their conversations.

Cultural Rites of Passage

There are cultural rites of passage that accompany any shift in culture. In his book *Transitions: Making Sense of Life's Changes* (1991). William Bridges writes, "Every transition begins with an ending" (p. 11). In Mark's case, the "garage sale" represented an ending or purge of the old and a new beginning. Robert Evans calls this stage in the change process "moving from loss to commitment" in his book *The Human Side of School Change* (1996, p. 61) and reminds us that we must tend to those who are finding themselves grieving through the loss, while also moving forward toward a new reality.

Cultural rites of passage can also be more subtle and involve less fanfare, but have an equally powerful impact on the school culture. At Cedar Way Elementary in Edmonds, Washington, principal Hawkins Cramer endeavored to lead his school through a four-year shift in how they were teaching literacy and math. Hawk's cultural rite of passage was to get into classrooms and teach lessons from the new curriculum. He put himself in the position of lead learner, and he'll tell you that a few of his lessons went very well (a good learning experience) and many others were flops (a better learning experience), and he sent the message that this is a new beginning for us all.

Michael Fullan (2001) reminds us that change takes time and effort, especially when changing a school's culture: "It is no doubt clear by now why there can never be a recipe or cookbook for change, nor a step-by-step process. Reculturing is a contact sport that involves hard, labor-intensive work. It takes time and indeed never ends" (p. xvii). Cultural rites of passage are but one step on the change continuum, but an important one to help individuals let go of the past and move toward the future.

The Role of Relationships

Crafting a school culture is also about the ways in which we relate with one another. This can be challenging when relationships are tied to emotion or personal philosophy, or are confrontational. These types of environments create a culture of *risk* in which teachers are reluctant to engage in shared learning and dialogue with colleagues. In this type of school or organizational climate, the first step is to create a safe environment in which members of the school community are willing to share their ideas and thinking with others.

Each of these schools illustrates the complex role of relationships in crafting a school culture. Karen's school was rich in kindness, and the teachers viewed themselves as friends as well as colleagues. In Mark's school, relationships among teachers were dominated by a few negative teachers who perceived their role as to fight against the "system." The teachers in Maria's school had a rather immediate bond due to the fact that so many were in their first few years of teaching. And in Marsha's school, relationships were at a social level and revolved around personal activities and interests. These examples are similar to the findings of Roland Barth and his work on relationships in schools. He writes (2006), "Relationships among educators within a school range from vigorously healthy to dangerously competitive. They might be categorized in four ways: parallel play, adversarial relationships, congenial relationships, and collegial relationships" (pp. 9–10). He goes on to share four ways that a school can create a culture rich in collegiality: "A precondition for doing *anything* to strengthen our practice and improve a school is the existence of a collegial culture in which professionals talk about practice, share their craft knowledge, and observe and root for the successes of one another" (p. 13).

Qualities of a School With a Culture of Learning

In spite of its grueling nature, there are many examples of schools that have tackled the mess of culture to create environments that maintain a culture of learning. By defining the outcomes we seek when crafting a culture of learning, we reinforce the concept that each and every member of our community has room for new knowledge and growth. It reinforces the reality that as educators, we *never* have it all figured out, which, if you ask me, is one of the greatest joys of being a teacher. Schools with a culture of learning share the following characteristics:

- The principal views him or herself as a learner.
- Data and student work guides decision making.
- The needs of the system are secondary to a focus on student learning.
- Time within the school day is provided for teachers to reflect as individuals, in small groups, or with a coach.
- Teachers are encouraged to examine a concept that directly relates to their students' learning over a period of time.
- Qualities and characteristics of adult learners are well understood and accounted for in designing professional development.
- There is a climate of trust where it is okay to make mistakes during the learning process.

Meanwhile . . . in the Principal's Office

When it comes to leading teacher learning, it sometimes feels like the classic dilemma of what comes first, the chicken or the egg? Should a school focus on developing the culture first and then engage teachers in coaching and professional development? Or does the act of engaging teachers in coaching and professional development create the school culture? The answer is quite simple: both are essential. We can create all the best professional development structures, hire the most effective coach, and carve out time for teachers to learn together, but without working on the culture we will fail to get the results we are hoping for. Conversely, we can focus all of our efforts on creating a learning-oriented culture through retreats and team-building activities, but without any structures in place for teacher learning, we won't get anywhere either.

This creates questions about the roles that the principal and coach play with regard to culture, and the following chart (Figure 3.1) defines how both can work together to collaboratively design and implement a system that addresses these factors.

Figure 3.1   Principal and Coach Roles for Crafting a Culture of Learning

The principal's role is to . . .
Maintain a learning stance
Manage and foster collegial relationships among the adults in the school by stating expectations explicitly, modeling collegiality, rewarding those who behave as colleagues, and protecting those who engage in collegial behaviors (Warren-Little, 1982)
Create time in the schedule for teachers to engage in meaningful conversations, reflection, and problem solving
Engage in the learning that is taking place among the teachers
Regularly share new learning, new thinking, and personal growth with others
Listen and respond to the ideas and concerns of others
Keep students' needs, rather than the teachers' needs, at the forefront of every conversation
Hold teachers accountable for being a productive part of the school community
Help teachers navigate through the change process
Set the tone that "we are all learners" and no one has it all figured out
Carefully craft messages and experiences that continually reinforce the goals and outcomes for student learning

(Continued)

Figure 3.1 (Continued)

The coach's role is to . . .
Maintain a learning stance
Build trust and relationships with teachers
Create opportunities for teachers to learn together, such as in coaching cycles, study groups, observations, and team meetings
Prioritize meaningful conversations, reflection, and problem solving when planning professional development—spend less time giving people information and more time helping them process through information
Avoid the trap of negativity—stay focused on the positive
Provide sustained and continuous support for teachers as they move through the change process
Keep students' needs, rather than the teachers' needs, at the forefront of every conversation
Listen and respond to the ideas and concerns of others

As a principal and coach team, take some time to have a conversation about your respective roles using the following questions:

- Which of these roles are we most comfortable with? Why?
- Which of these roles are we least comfortable with? Why?
- What forms of support will we each need to enact these roles?
- How will we check in with each other about our progress and challenges?

The Question of Evaluation and Confidentiality

In almost every session with coaches, the question of evaluation and confidentiality is raised. This tends to be of great concern among coaches who are new to the field as they face the prospect of building trust with a staff of teachers for the first time. They worry that they will be perceived as a spy for the principal and are greatly concerned about how they might be thought of by their peers. This becomes less of an issue as coaches get more experience, because relationships are established and trust is in place.

When it comes to evaluation and confidentiality, some coaching models take the approach that nothing at all is to be shared with the principal. Others defer to the teacher to determine what will be shared. In my opinion, both of these approaches reinforce privatization within a school culture—something that coaching can be designed to counteract.

There is a fine balance regarding what is shared between the coach and principal. To accomplish this we need to carefully create a system that maintains trust but also provides the information the principal needs as the school leader. Discussing the following questions as a principal and coach team will guide this conversation:

- In what ways has trust been established? Where is the coach in the process of building relationships with teachers?
- What work still needs to be done regarding building trust?
- How will the principal and coach share specific information about the teaching and learning?
- How often and in what ways will the principal spend time in classrooms to get a personal perspective of how things are going?
- What coaching notes and materials will be shared with the principal?
- How will this information be shared with teachers?

Tools and Techniques

Karen's school provided many rich examples of friendship and kindness and fewer examples of collegiality and rigorous dialogue and communication. According to Jim Knight (2007),

> Communicating an important message can be one of the most authentic, rewarding experiences in life. When we communicate, we learn; share thoughts, experiences, and emotions; and become colleagues, friends, and soul mates. Words and language, messages sent and received, can build a tie between people that is deep, strong, and even lifelong. Effective communication can enable the kind of faithful relationship that we build our lives around. Unfortunately, words can also destroy relationships. A simple innocent comment can do damage that may take years to repair, or damage that may never be repaired. Getting our message through is a messy business. (p. 58)

Tackling how the faculty communicated was an important first step, and Karen turned to the Seven Norms of Collaborative Work (Figure 3.2) as a tool for growth and reflection in this area.

Figure 3.2   The Seven Norms of Collaborative Work in Action

Norm	What It Looks Like in Action
1. Pausing	*In Group Work:*
Pausing before responding allows time for thinking and enhances dialogue, discussion, and decision making.	Group members engage thoughtfully in the conversation by taking time to think and reflect before responding. This requires participants to slow down, listen, and weigh the thoughts of others before sharing their own thinking. To promote this behavior, the facilitator may use practices such as reflective writing/journaling at specific points in the conversation, reminding group members to resist the temptation to solve a problem right away, and using protocols that build in time for each person to contribute.
	In Coaching Conversations:
	The coach listens attentively to the teacher before responding with the "right" answer. The coach also recognizes that coaching conversations are more meaningful when both the teacher and coach are provided with the opportunity to share their knowledge and ideas over time, such as through coaching cycles.
2. Paraphrasing	*In Group Work:*
Paraphrasing allows us to hear and understand each other as we evolve in our thinking.	When a lack of clarity exists about what is being shared by a colleague, participants regularly paraphrase what was said and seek confirmation that the message of the listener is being understood. Examples of paraphrasing stems include "I think what I'm hearing you say is . . ." or "It sounds like you are saying . . ."
	In Coaching Conversations:
	The same strategy readily applies to coaching conversations. Using similar stems, the coach may paraphrase what was shared to confirm that the teacher was understood and move the thinking forward.
3. Probing	*In Group Work:*
Using gentle, open-ended probes or inquiries increases clarity and precision of a person's thinking.	Group members regularly probe one another to enhance the overall learning of the group. Probing is honest and open-minded, and has the sole purpose of clarifying and enhancing the work of the group. Examples of probing stems include "Please say more . . ." or "Can you tell me about . . ." or "Then, are you saying . . . ?" Effective probing does not include leading questions, questions that are driven by a personal agenda, or suggestions that are disguised as questions.

Norm	What It Looks Like in Action
	In Coaching Conversations:
	When used effectively, probing is a nonthreatening process that deepens and extends the learning of both the teacher and coach. Examples of probing stems for coaching are "Why do you think the students responded in this way?" "Tell me more about this . . ." "What can we learn from the student work to enhance our thinking?" "I'd love to hear your thinking on this, tell me more . . ."
4. Putting Ideas on the Table	*In Group Work:*
Sharing ideas are the heart of meaningful dialogue. However, one must remain open-minded and thoughtful in relation to the ideas that are being shared by oneself and others.	Group members understand that there are many solutions to any given problem and are encouraged to toss a variety of ideas on the table during a conversation. Examples are "Here is one idea . . ." or "One thought I have is . . ." or "Here is a possible approach . . ." or "I'm just thinking out loud . . ."
	In Coaching Conversations:
	In order to validate and learn from teachers, coaches begin most conversations by soliciting ideas from the teacher before sharing their own ideas. Later in the conversation, a coach may share an idea or two using the following stems: "One thing that might make sense is . . ." or "What do you think about . . ."
5. Paying Attention to Self and Others	*In Group Work:*
Meaningful dialogue is facilitated when we are aware of both what we are saying as well as how others are responding to what is being said.	Group members demonstrate this norm by staying conscious of how their behavior affects the group. For example, group members who may choose to speak too often or not often enough in group settings. By making a group aware of this norm, participants learn to adapt their behavior accordingly.
	In Coaching Conversations:
	Coaching conversations, like all conversations, are a back-and-forth dialogue in which the two people listen, respond, and adapt to one another. By paying attention to self and others, the coach adjusts throughout the conversation, and may do so by drawing upon other norms, including pausing, probing, and paraphrasing.

(Continued)

Figure 3.2 (Continued)

Norm	What It Looks Like in Action
6. *Presuming Positive Intentions*	*In Group Work:*
Assuming that a colleague's comments, questions, or statements are coming from a positive place promotes and facilitates productive dialogue and eliminates unintentional resentment, hurt feelings, and misunderstandings.	Though group members may disagree with a colleague, the underlying sentiment is that they believe that the intentions of that person are positive. Groups that don't demonstrate this norm bring judgments and negative viewpoints of their colleagues into group dialogue. Groups that demonstrate this norm may use the following stems: "I appreciate what you are saying . . ." "What you are saying makes sense because . . ." "I understand that with your background, this is how you view the situation. However . . ."
	In Coaching Conversations:
	Coaching is driven by respectful and trusting relationships, and when a coach carries a negative view of a teacher, it shows. Coaches who demonstrate this norm are open-minded about both the teachers with whom they collaborate as well as how any given problem might be solved.
7. *Pursuing a Balance Between Advocacy and Inquiry*	*In Group Work:*
Maintaining a balance between advocating for a position and questioning one's own position assists the group in becoming a learning organization.	We all carry baggage, and groups are no different. Effective groups refrain from pushing a personal agenda and instead regularly question their position throughout the learning process.
	In Coaching Conversations:
	Coaches also benefit from maintaining a position of inquiry in their work with teachers. Even in situations where the coach's role is to promote a specific program or curriculum, there is still room to question and analyze. When we approach coaching myopically—or as there being one way of doing things—we've lost sight of this norm.

Adapted from Bill Baker Group Dynamics, Berkeley.

Consultancy Protocol

Marsha's school found the Consultancy Protocol (Figure 3.3) to be a useful tool for adding structure to conversations and keeping the teachers focused. For more examples of protocols, see the Resources.

Figure 3.3   The Consultancy Protocol

Purpose: This protocol is used to explore a problem or dilemma related to teaching and learning. (Suggested time: 45–60 minutes)

Roles:

- *Presenting group member* shares a dilemma for the group to discuss
- *Participants* listen, reflect, and discuss the dilemma that is shared
- *Facilitator* manages the process, keeps on eye on the time, and encourages everyone to participate in the discussion

Process:

1. The presenting group member shares an issue or dilemma. If possible, the issue is presented in the form of a focus question (5 minutes).
2. The facilitator restates the issue or dilemma to ensure that it is clear and well understood (1–2 minutes).
3. Participants ask clarifying questions to be sure they understand the context and history of the issue or dilemma. The presenting group member responds to the questions to provide more context and background (5–10 minutes).

   Note: Clarifying questions are aimed at helping the participants understand the issue or dilemma and are not a place to make suggestions.
4. Participants ask probing questions. The presenting group member responds to the group's questions to continue adding context and background (5–10 minutes).

   Note: Probing questions are deeper than clarifying questions but still are not suggestions.
5. The presenting group member listens and takes notes while the participants discuss the issue or dilemma that was presented (10–15 minutes).
6. The presenting group member responds to the discussion and thoughtfully reflects on his or her next steps (5 minutes).
7. The group engages in an open discussion and debriefs the process (5–10 minutes).

Assessing Your School Culture

The following benchmarks and indicators serve as a tool to measure, discuss, and set goals for your school in terms of climate and culture. By reflecting on the following attributes, a principal and coach team can plan next steps for crafting a school culture, much like the schools did that were highlighted in this chapter. Attributes of an effective school culture include the following:

- *Benchmark I.* Members of the school community hold one another accountable through open, honest, and trusting dialogue.
  - Leadership understands the challenges of teaching but also encourages efforts at improvement.

- o Experimentation is encouraged and shared.
- o Mistakes are viewed as part of the learning process.
- o Teachers are able to challenge the school leadership and vice versa.
- o Dialogue is at the collegial level.

- *Benchmark II.* Professional development is aligned and focused on one area of improvement at a time.
  - o Professional development is organized across the three venues of large group, small group, and one-on-one support.
  - o There is a clear and well-understood learning focus for teachers.
  - o The learning focus comes from student work and/or data.
  - o The learning focus is determined by the faculty to ensure that there is a sense of shared ownership for the work.

- *Benchmark III.* Collaboration among the principal, teachers, and coach is grounded in student work.
  - o Conversations about teaching and learning are shaped by student work.
  - o Well-designed processes and protocols guide the use of student work.
  - o Teachers are held accountable to apply what is learned in these conversations with their students. (Student work can include students' written work; formal and informal assessment data; and anecdotal records such as conference notes, running records, and other student observations.)

- *Benchmark IV.* Focused and rigorous collaboration takes place on a consistent basis.
  - o Skilled facilitator(s) manage the collaboration process.
  - o Teachers are skilled group members and understand how to collaborate effectively.
  - o There is a broad array of collaboration processes in use (protocols, norms, etc.).

- *Benchmark V.* Members of the school community are provided time and resources to engage in learning. Learning is expected.
  - o The school leader and coach view themselves as learners.
  - o The school leadership and coach understand that teachers are not "fixed" but rather are encouraged to be active participants in the learning process.

o The school leadership and coach are skilled at supporting teachers as learners.

- *Benchmark VI.* Members of the school community support and encourage one another, both publicly and privately.

  o Members of the school community are not adversarial or competitive.
  o Teachers, the principal, and coach look for opportunities to share the successes of every colleague.
  o There is a platform for sharing successes, such as in a faculty meeting, in a weekly bulletin, in grade-level meetings, and in department meetings.
  o Certain teachers aren't "favored" over others. Rather, the successes of all teachers are shared.

- *Benchmark VII.* Members of the school community observe one another with the purpose of sharing practices, asking questions, and considering teaching dilemmas.

  o There is an established structure for classroom observations (see Chapter 4).
  o All teachers are provided with the opportunity to participate as hosts or observers in learning labs.
  o A skilled facilitator manages the learning lab process.

- *Benchmark VIII.* Members of the school community pursue and share key learnings from external professional development opportunities.

  o Resources are set aside for members of the school community to participate in outside professional development opportunities, such as conferences, workshops, and observations in other schools.
  o Those who participate in outside professional development share their key learnings with colleagues.

- *Benchmark IX.* Members of the school community are supported through student-centered coaching.

  o Coaching provides teachers with ongoing and need-based support.
  o Teachers determine the focus for the coaching.
  o Coaching is driven by student work.
  o Coaching is based on a six- to nine-week cycle.

A Final Thought

I used to think about coaching as a stand-alone solution for teacher learning. Then I realized how much climate and culture shape the outcomes of coaching. This came to me after several experiences where I was working with committed coaches in schools that hadn't yet developed a learning culture. Issues around climate and culture made their work near-to-impossible and deepened my understanding about how important culture is if we want coaching to impact students and teachers. We cannot allow the existing culture to be our default but instead we must think critically about how to positively influence our school culture so that our students perform at the highest levels.

The fact that no two schools are alike is demonstrated by the schools that are highlighted in this chapter. Each school reflected on the status quo and responded with explicit steps to craft a school culture that adapted and responded to the needs of the students. Steps that a single individual wouldn't have been able to implement. Steps that took the collaboration of a principal and coach team.

Section II

Data as an Essential Component of Student-Centered Coaching

4

Data and Student-Centered Coaching

Data is fundamental to student-centered coaching. It moves the coaching conversation away from what a teacher and coach *think* the teacher should be doing and focuses it on using student evidence to determine what they now know the teacher *can* be doing to improve student achievement.

Not too long ago, data played a minor role in guiding curriculum and instruction. Decisions were based on arbitrary ideas about what to teach and were often grounded more on personal philosophy than on student learning targets. Today, districts face federal and local requirements to use a narrow array of assessments in ways that may not readily inform instruction either. Consequently, many educators have never discovered the true power of data. In this chapter, we will see how teachers can take a fresh look at using data to reach their goals for student learning.

Why Use Data?

As teachers use data in meaningful ways, they become aware of the many opportunities there are to tap into the rich array of information that surrounds them on a daily basis. They are able to draw from what students know and are able to do instead of marching through a prepared set of lessons that may or may not meet their students' needs. In the report titled *Making the Most of Interim Assessment Data,* Christman et al. write,

> The logic behind how interim assessment data can assist teachers is straightforward: a teacher acquires data about what her students have learned; she examines the data to see where her students are strong and weak; she custom-tailors what and how she teaches so that individuals and groups of students learn more; and as teachers across the school engage in this process, the school as a whole improves. (2009, p. 5)

Student evidence, or data, includes any information that helps us understand where the students are in their learning. It can focus on academics, student behavior, or classroom community, and it may include written assignments, student notes, behaviors, verbal statements, or anything else that we see or hear students doing. Student evidence can be collected through formal or informal assessments, conferences, observations, or just talking with kids. It can be hard for teachers to manage so much information, yet the richer the array of student evidence we use, the better our instruction.

Coaching in Data-Driven Schools

A gap exists in our schools, separating the data that surrounds teachers on a daily basis from how (or whether) they use it. This "data gap" is commonly due to an overabundance of data, a lack of systems to analyze data, or limited experience among teachers in using data, and can be significantly reduced through coaching conversations that are rooted in student evidence.

I recently visited a suburban, high-achieving school district to shadow Tony, a math coach, as he worked with a group of kindergarten teachers at the beginning of the school year. The district used a reliable math assessment that was administered with each student in the first few weeks of school. At Tony's request, the teachers brought their students' data for today's planning conversation.

Tony had facilitated teams in this school for years. Some teams were comfortable using data to tackle the dilemmas they faced as teachers. He found that with these teams, he simply reminded teachers to bring student evidence and they were able to dive right in. Other teams weren't quite there yet. They were anxious about using data and viewed Tony as someone who stirs the pot. Right in the middle were teams like the one he was working with today: hard-working, creative, and committed teachers who were interested in doing what was best for their students but weren't used to planning with data. With this in mind, Tony was careful to put the data front and center while honoring what the teachers had done in the past. He began the conversation by asking, "Thanks for bringing your math data with you today. What did you learn about your students from the math assessment?" Sarah, a second-year teacher, jumped right in and said, "I'm pleased because the math assessment shows that most of my students have a pretty good understanding of number recognition and counting, and many are able to write their numbers up to 10." Sue agreed, "I found the same thing with my class." "Me, too," agreed Becca.

Gradually the conversation shifted to what their approach would be for teaching math over the next four weeks. Sue, a veteran teacher, said, "I have a great unit that I like to do at the beginning of the school year. I use math manipulatives and have a lot of math games already prepared." She pointed to a shelf in the corner with neatly organized bins of dice, game boards, and other manipulatives. "I've shared these with Sarah and Becca, and we think the kids will love them."

Tony recognized that Sue was a leader on the team and wanted to respect her and honor her ideas. But he also wanted to help the teachers connect their instruction with the data that was in front of them. His mind was racing about how to do both, and he asked, "Math games are a terrific way to teach conceptual understanding. I'm wondering what the goals are for the students as they engage in these activities? It might be a good idea to think about this as we take a look at your materials. Let's make a list . . ." and he wrote on a large piece of chart paper, "Students will . . ."

Sue jumped up to pull several plastic bins from the shelf, spread the games on the table, and began explaining, "This game is great for filling in missing numbers in a sequence. This is a dice game for the students to practice writing their numbers."

Tony gave the group some time to look through and discuss the games, and then he returned to the chart and said, "Well these look great; let's see what we can figure out for our student goals."

The teachers looked from the table covered in materials, to the chart, and then to Tony, and after several seconds, Sarah said, "Well . . . I think we could write, 'Students will learn number sense' because a lot of the games focus on counting and writing numbers." The others agreed and Tony wrote the goal on the chart.

Then Becca added, "We could say, 'Students will learn how to write numbers in the correct order.'"

Sue had been quiet during this part of the conversation and then said, "To be honest, I'm a little bit worried. Now that I see the goals for students and think back to our assessment data, I'm wondering if these games are too easy for our kids. They seem to focus on what the students already know."

Tony had been thinking the same thing. He was happy to hear Sue raise the question and suggested, "If number sense is our goal, then why don't we look at the district's unit on number sense, check the standards, and plan from there? I think we may find that when we look at the assessment data against the standards and curriculum, we'll have a clearer sense of what we should do next. I'm also guessing we can use many of these games with the students who need more support." The teachers agreed and pulled out their calendars to set the next meeting.

As Tony headed back to his office, he felt a sense of relief that the data raised this question and he didn't have to. His work with this team was just getting started and now they had a focus for their weekly meetings. Sarah and Becca also indicated an interest in pairing up for a coaching cycle focused on teaching number sense. And Sue requested help from Tony on an informal basis just to be sure she was on the right track. Tony had done what he set out to do with this team—he had helped them begin to see the power within the data. Figure 4.1 details how Tony structured his conversation with the kindergarten team.

Figure 4.1   Data-Driven Coaching Conversations

1. Identify key findings from relevant assessment data. What are the students' strengths and needs as determined by the data?

2. Look to the standards and curriculum to determine a focus for future instruction. What are the goals for student learning using the language, "Students will . . ."?

3. Plan how the students' needs will be addressed through differentiated instruction. How will we deliver instruction that meets the needs of all students?

4. Reassess student learning on a regular basis (formally or informally) to determine if instruction is meeting their needs. If it isn't, adjust the instructional practices that are being used with students.

During this conversation, Tony took an important step to narrow the data gap. In the past, the math assessment had been given to students, turned in, and forgotten. But by using the data in a practical way, it became relevant. And by asking the teachers to write "Students will . . . " statements alongside the assessment data, Tony redirected the teachers to connect the assessment data to their lesson plans, helping them rethink how they would design their math instruction to meet the needs not just of a *generic* group of kindergartners but for *this group* of kindergartners. He was also careful to find a meaningful way to continue using some of the materials that the teachers had already prepared and were excited about, so that his relationships with the teachers would continue to thrive.

A Case Study in Using Data:
Denver School of Science and Technology

At the Denver School of Science and Technology (DSST), teachers and school leaders have developed a framework for creating a responsive and assessment-driven school culture that requires teachers to set clear targets for learning, measure progress with consistent monitoring of student learning, and analyze student data in relationship to the targets (Figure 4.2).

Figure 4.2 A Framework for Data-Driven Schools

Stage One:	Stage Two:	Stage Three:	Stage Four:
Set clear learning targets for students that are based on the standards.	Continually assess students (formally and informally) through daily, weekly, and monthly assessments that measure progress towards the learning targets.	Build in time and systems for teams to analyze data and adapt instruction to address students' needs.	Continually collect data to chart students' growth and analyze the validity and impact of the instructional practices.
Guiding questions	**Guiding questions**	**Guiding questions**	**Guiding questions**
- What should the students learn? - What knowledge and skills will they be able to demonstrate on the assessments?	- How can we design assessments to provide data on how the students are progressing toward the learning targets? - How will we manage and organize the data?	- Where do we see evidence of student learning and/or mastery? - Where do we see gaps? - How will we address these gaps?	- Where do we see evidence of student learning and/or mastery? - Where do we see gaps? - How will we address these gaps? - What must we do to ensure that all students reach mastery of standards by the end of the year?

A charter, open-enrollment public school serving middle and high school students, DSST's use of data to drive instruction has been a key leverage point for student growth and achievement. Admittedly, DSST is a secondary school that lies outside of what we view as typical or traditional. Yet, I've decided to introduce the data practices that are used in this school because they are getting results with students. And also because it is a model that, with attention, can broadly transfer across the K–12 spectrum.

Mariah Dickson serves as the director of curriculum and assessment for DSST Public Schools. In her role, Mariah serves in both an administrative and coaching capacity to set out performance measures for teachers and to help teachers meet these performance goals. Mariah calls this model "performance coaching" because she sets high standards for teachers and then provides the necessary support to help them meet these standards. In some schools, a blended role in which the coach serves in both an administrative and coaching capacity would be less than effective. But since DSST is a school that is driven by accountability and performance indicators, this blended role is effective in setting high standards and also providing the necessary support to teachers.

Mariah describes the process at DSST as "dogged and long-term work." It hasn't been easy but it is worth it as the school—with a student population that has 45% students qualifying for free and reduced lunch—has been named the highest performing school in Denver with 100% of the first three graduating classes (Class of 2008, 2009, and 2010) admitted to four-year colleges/universities with more minority and low-income students than from any school in the state. Forty percent of students in the Class of 2009 were the first from their families to attend college.

At DSST, standards and assessment data are at the core of all instructional decision making. Their Instructional Model (Figure 4.3) sets forth a process for teachers to use a variety of assessments (daily mastery checks, weekly formative assessments, end-of-unit assessments, and final exams) to directly measure the standards. All lesson plans and curriculum maps are built around the standards, and teachers code the assessments by a standards tracking system to measure student progress and adapt instruction accordingly.

Led by the principal and the director of curriculum and assessment, teachers participate in the process of ongoing reflection to maximize student learning. The process adheres to the following framework:

Figure 4.3 DSST Instructional Model

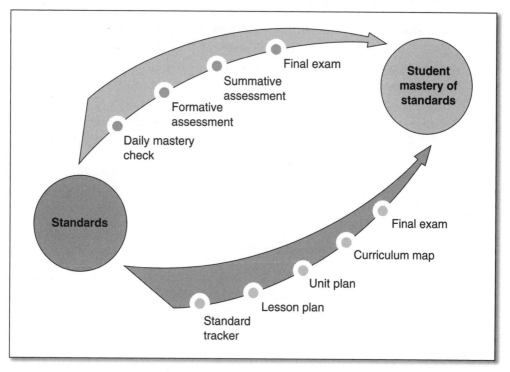

Start With a Clear (and Measurable) Set of Standards, and Stick to These Standards

Early on, the teachers at DSST found the Colorado State Standards too vague to adequately measure where students were on any given day. With direction from the administrative team, each department worked collaboratively to rework the standards into more specific and measurable components. For example, "making inferences" was broken down into more specific standards such as "making inferences about the character using evidence from the text." With this level of specificity, the standards could more easily be assessed and the teachers could pinpoint specific problems to immediately design and implement strategies to address these problems.

As you might imagine, making decisions about what *specifically* the teachers wanted the students to master wasn't easy. It has been grit-your-teeth-and-roll-up-your-sleeves kind of work that has called upon teachers to come together to make difficult decisions about what they think the students should learn in any given subject and grade level.

All Curriculum and Assessments Are Built on Standards

Teachers at DSST implement a core set of instructional practices that ensure the use of data occurs on a daily basis. And since the approach to data-driven instruction is a schoolwide expectation, there are structures in place to ensure it is fully implemented. Teachers complete (and turn in) lessons plans (Figure 4.4) and code the instruction based on whether the standard is something the students will be exposed to (E) or will gain mastery of (M), or if it is something they are

Figure 4.4   Lesson Plan Template

Denver School of Science and Technology Lesson Plan					
Teacher(s): **Dates:** **Course:**			**Grade:**		
	Monday	*Tuesday*	*Wednesday*	*Thursday*	*Friday*
Standards: Code as Exposure (E), Mastery (M), or Spiral (S)					
Vocabulary					
Assessment of Mastery					
Classroom Routines Do Now Learning Activities Mastery Check					
Homework					
Materials/Notes (Optional)					

reviewing as part of a spiraling approach (S). They also build into their plans relevant vocabulary and how they will assess learning, classroom routines, and homework. Teachers and students track student mastery against the standards through daily mastery checks. On a recent visit, I observed a class of freshman algebra students recording their progress toward the specific standards they had been working on for the past week. There was no question about the grades students were receiving or where they stood in relationship to the standards—they were keeping track right along with the teacher.

Professional Development Is Tied to Data and Assessment

Analyzing student assessment data and planning instruction is the predominant professional development approach at DSST. The collaborative use of data occurs in weekly teacher planning meetings, in grade-level teams, in department meetings, and during intensive data analysis and planning sessions that occur at the end of each trimester. In most cases, the sessions are facilitated by the department chairs, providing teachers with the help they need to analyze student data to determine what steps to take to ensure that the students are moving toward mastery.

Professional development also provides teachers with support to implement a core set of instructional practices (DSST Core Instructional Practices) based on cognitive brain research, including a decrease in a lecture-style delivery of content and an increase in written response and discussion, differentiation, and scaffolding instruction. A walk through the school illustrates the depth and scope of the implementation of these practices as they are truly in place in each and every classroom.

The Work Has Been Done *by* Teachers and Not *to* Teachers

A goal at DSST is to create self-sustaining teams that manage their own learning. The school vision is set forth by the administrative team and the process of how to get there is managed by the teachers. This creates a school culture where teachers are expected to work together to see the vision through to fruition. Mariah Dickson explains,

We work with the teachers to decide how to best meet the needs of the students and they figure out how to make it happen. The more steps that they design, the more owner-ship they have. As administrators, we design the process, and as teachers, they implement it in their classrooms.

Coaching With Student Data

The emphasis in using data at DSST involves a collaborative effort among department chairs, teachers, and the school leadership. In many cases, a school-based coach is responsible for organizing and creating dialogue about assessment data. Some coaches feel intimidated about bringing data into conversations with teachers because they fear data will make teachers feel nervous or threatened. But when coaches take a student-centered approach, the use of data and student work becomes a natural (and expected) part of the process and teachers often claim that, as a result of the focus on students, coaching feels less personal. The following coaching practices are nonthreatening and are based on creating a culture that collaborates around data.

Sorting for Differentiation

Sorting student evidence, such as recent tests, written responses, or other assignments, helps a coach and teacher recognize patterns and trends related to student learning. In Chapter 1, you read about sorting student work with Kristi, a middle school teacher. Kristi had a three-part goal for her students and we sorted the students' written responses against the goal. By doing so, we were able to determine which students were thinking deeply as they read, which needed a few more strategies to use while reading, and which were not showing any evidence of the goal. In a 30-minute planning session, we were able to assess the students and design a differentiated plan for instruction based on the student evidence.

When sorting student work, I suggest making three piles of work that have similar attributes. That way, you are less tempted to only celebrate the masterpieces or become consumed by the work that is below par. The process is led by the goal(s) for student learning and we use these simple questions to guide the process, "How do the student work samples compare to the goals we set for students? And, what will we do next to address the students' needs?"

Data Teams and Assessment Walls

After winding through the corridors of Franklin Elementary, I open the door to room 122 and realize I've found the right place when I see pocket charts lining the walls of the unused classroom—each with slips of colorful paper peeking out of the small translucent pockets. It's a cold January morning and I've come to observe Mary, the literacy coach, as she leads teams of teachers through their second assessment wall meeting of the year.

Mary arrives and says, "I'm so glad you made it. Our first team will be coming soon . . . it includes all three of the third-grade teachers along with the ELL and special education teacher. Then we'll repeat that schedule with two other teams. They are released for a 60-minute block and I'll continue on with the rest tomorrow. We should also see the principal attending most of the meetings . . . if she doesn't get pulled out for something."

"Sounds great," I respond. "Is it okay if I sit over here and listen and take notes?" "Sure," she says, "but I'd love to get your feedback after the session if you don't mind."

I'm not surprised to hear this request. I've worked with Mary for two years and have always been struck by the depth of reflection she brings to her work as a literacy coach. "Of course," I say. "Do you mind if I ask what you hope to accomplish today? Do you have the same goals for each team or are the teams in different places?"

After a moment she answers, "My goal for all of the sessions is for the teachers to really see where their students are and think together about what to do next. I also hope to engage the ELL and special education teachers into the conversations so that we can create a plan for serving the students that includes everyone."

As she says this, the school principal arrives. Heather has cleared her schedule to be here because she has set a personal goal to know each and every student in the school. She is a relatively new principal, in her second year, and she recognizes that listening to these conversations is a great opportunity because it helps her learn more about the students and know how their needs are being addressed as well.

A young teacher enters the room and Mary introduces us. Sandy is in her first year. She unloads an armful of notebooks and takes a seat next to me. The others come in and are chatting and laughing. They include Scott and Kathy, the other two third-grade teachers, and Natalia (ELL) and Martha (special education).

Mary knows she has a lot to cover and gets started. She quickly introduces me and explains to the teachers that my role is to provide training and support to the literacy coaches throughout the district.

She invites the teachers to speak freely and reminds them that student confidentially will be maintained. (Note: Student names have been changed for their privacy.)

Then she smiles and says, "Okay, guys, where are our kids today? Why don't we get started moving the cards?" The team knows that she is referring to the recent Development Reading Assessment (DRA) that was administered to the students the week prior. At Franklin, the DRA is administered two times a year—in August and January—which provides data for the assessment wall meetings that are held in each of these months.

The teachers pull out the data sheets they were asked to bring and take turns at the charts pulling cards, each representing a different student, and moving them between the pockets that are denoted with the DRA reading levels. When I look closely, I notice that some of the cards are marked with stickers to identify whether the students are served by special education, ELL, or another intervention such as Reading Recovery or after-school tutoring.

After a few minutes, the teachers settle back into their chairs and Mary says, "Let's go through our outliers." With direction from the district, Franklin has established a range for where the third graders should be at this point in the year (between DRA levels 24 and 38), and these cut points are visibly marked on the pocket charts. Outliers are the students who are either above or below this range.

Scott says, "I'll start. Carson is at the DRA level 20. He is having a hard time focusing—he pinballs around the classroom and has been struggling during independent reading. I could use some help with how to move him forward. I also have four ELL students who have fallen behind where they used to be. Natalia—correct me if I'm wrong—but I think they were tested in Spanish the first time and this time they were tested in English because they are being transitioned. I'm not sure what to do about that. And for my outliers on the other end, I have Antoine who is a level 40. I'm worried that he might be getting bored because his behavior is a little bit iffy lately. My problem is I don't have a high enough reading group for him."

As Scott talks through his students, Mary creates a list on the whiteboard alongside the pocket charts, writing the following:

High Outliers	Low Outliers	ELL Needs
Antoine (40)	Carson (20)	Rubia (16)
		Natasha (14)
		Servando (18)
		Javier (12)

After each of the teachers shares, the conversation turns to what to do to help the students advance as readers. They tackle Scott's students first and then move on to the students in the other classrooms. Kathy says, "You know, Scott, I have a reading group that is right about at Antoine's level. Why don't you send him into my room for the reading block?"

"That would be great. He would love that and I think your kids would be great models for him," says Scott. Mary makes a note on the back of Antoine's card to note this change in his instructional plan.

"As far as the ELL kids go," says Natalia, "there are many who are transitioning at this time of the year. It might make sense for me to reassess them in Spanish reading and then also give them an assessment on their oral English just to be sure they are getting the right services. After I do that, we should talk about the types of interventions that make sense for them."

"And for Carson," says Martha, "here's what I think. He's definitely struggled lately to stay focused. His IEP meeting is in a few weeks but I don't want to wait for that. Let me see if I can work my schedule to push in during the reading block and sit with him."

Scott nods and adds, "That would be great but I think there are other things I can do with him too. Can we brainstorm some ideas next time we meet?"

For today, their time is almost up and Mary suggests, "Okay, guys, let's talk about our next steps. How about if we agree to come back together during our regular team meeting to think about the ELL students when we have more assessment data. And we can also check in about the other students we discussed, like Carson." The teachers nod, gather their things, and rush off to greet their students.

"Whew," I say to Mary. "What a process. How do you feel about it?" Mary thinks for a moment and says, "I think I accomplished what I had hoped for. The teachers really know their kids and they created a plan to meet their needs. I feel good about that." Heather and I nod just as the next batch of teachers begins to file in. Figure 4.5 on the following page provides a protocol for assessment wall conversations.

Data teams and assessment walls serve as a vehicle for charting student progress and deepening discourse among teachers to propel student learning. Originally attributed to the work of Dorn and Soffos (2001), assessment walls employ all types of data to measure progress among the greater student population in order to nudge student performance from the private domain of grade books to a public, and open, discussion about student learning.

Figure 4.5   Before, During, and After the Assessment Wall Meeting at Franklin Elementary

Before the Assessment Wall Meeting

1. The school determines how often the assessment wall meetings will take place, which areas will be tracked, the assessment(s) that will be used, and what the target range will be that corresponds to the assessment wall meetings.

2. The coach creates the assessment wall using pocket charts, bulletin boards, or even a digital format such as a SMART Board.

3. At specific points in the year, the teachers assess their students and pull together the data into a usable form, such as a spreadsheet or table.

4. During the assessment wall meeting, the teachers move the students' cards to the location that matches the current assessment data.

5. The teachers discuss the "outliers," or students who fall outside the target range.

6. The teachers and support staff create a plan that leverages all the school's resources and personnel.

7. The coach records the actions that were taken as well as next steps.

After the Assessment Wall Meeting

8. The coach maintains the assessment wall, incrementally moving the range forward to match the goals set by the school or district.

9. The coach ensures that the conversation is followed up on and provides the necessary support to teachers and students.

The National Staff Development Council writes, "Another benefit of data analysis, particularly the examination of student work, is that the study of such evidence is itself a potent means of staff development. Teachers who use one of several group processes available for the study of student work report that the ensuing discussions of the assignment, the link between the work and content standards, their expectations for student learning, and the use of scoring rubrics improve their teaching and student learning" (NSDC Standards).

The work that schools do with assessment walls is only as good as the learning targets, and as it is at DSST, an important first step is to refine the student objectives before engaging in a conversation about how the students are doing in relationship to these targets. Once the targets are in place, the act of moving students along the continuum helps teachers think more clearly about how the students are performing as learners. Coding students based on classifications such as English-language learner, special education, gifted, and on the interventions they have received, brings to light trends and patterns that the teachers may otherwise overlook.

Pamela Schaff, one of three instructional coaches at Valhalla Elementary in the Federal Way Public Schools, describes their assessment wall as follows:

Valhalla's assessment wall for reading (Figure 4.6) is a visual tracking system to monitor the progress of our students who are below or approaching grade-level standards. Teachers update color-coded strips of paper on the wall based on student running record scores and reading inventories. Each child's reading slip is saved each year and updated with data four times a year. This allows us to see the reading journey of each child in our school. Colored strips are used to represent children who are qualified for special education and English-language learner (ELL) programs. Each ELL child also has a colored dot to represent the child's language proficiency level. This allows us to stay cognizant of the child's growth in the four domains of language acquisition when the child is struggling to make the district standard. In October, January, March, and June, each grade level gathers around the wall to move each student's strip. The purpose is to visually track the growth as well as to zero in on those children who are not making the necessary gains as readers. The black dividers

Figure 4.6 Valhalla's Reading Assessment Wall

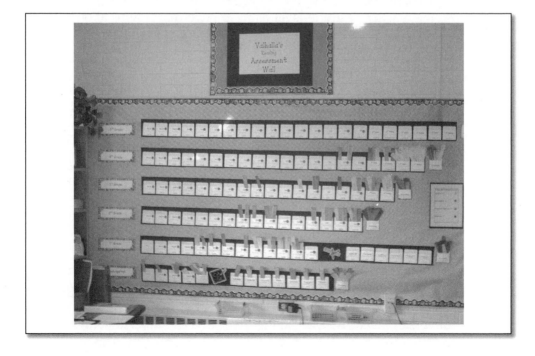

show the current grade-level standard for below, approaching, and meeting. The stars at the end of each row show the percentage of students who are meeting or exceeding the standard. This process is a great opportunity for celebrating the progress children are making but also a perfect springboard for discussion about what we need to do to move children to the next level. Teachers are aware of the needs of their individual students and the progress each child is making. The assessment wall is a vehicle for ensuring that every staff member is taking ownership of every child and his or her needs at every grade level.

After all slips have been updated and moved, support staff (instructional coach, ELL teacher, and interventionist), principal, and the grade-level team begin by celebrating the success of the children at a specific grade level. The team then looks at the students who are not meeting the grade-level standard and discusses what they see and hear getting in the way of these children, such as language acquisition, attendance, meeting IEP goals but not district standard, instruction not being focused enough, teacher unsure of next steps for child, and so on. The support staff and principal then offer to meet with the teachers individually or as a team to further modify and enhance the instruction, gather and discuss needed resources, and support the needs of individual teachers or grade-level teams as appropriate. Instructional coaches, interventionists, the ELL teacher, and the principal then continue to meet with the teacher or grade-level team to have discussions about the progress each child is or isn't making on a monthly basis. This often opens the door for a coaching opportunity.

Valhalla also has an assessment wall for math in Grades 3–5 to monitor student progress in computational fluency as well as the district assessment that must be passed to ensure promotion to the next grade level. Teachers update it in a similar fashion as the reading wall. Additionally, ELL students are monitored in each of the four domains of language acquisition (reading, writing, listening, and speaking). The four domains, level of language acquisition, and grade level divide the data wall in a manner that monitors the ELL students' growth (Figure 4.7). Conversations and instructional implications are then discussed, implemented, and monitored as needed.

Pam is an experienced coach and has worked for several years with her team to implement and refine the assessment wall process. She and the other coaches have found that what happens in conversations at the assessment wall directly impacts the rest of the coaching work that takes place with teachers, making it an invaluable

Figure 4.7   Valhalla's Four Domains of Language Assessment Wall

process. The soil for coaching is continually being tilled and creates opportunities for Pam and the other coaches to tap into the needs that arise through one-on-one coaching and small-group collaboration.

As the principal at Valhalla, Marie Verhaar has shown her dedication to raising student achievement by developing systems, like the assessment wall, for teachers to come together to think critically about how they can better meet the needs of all students. Under her leadership, Valhalla was the first school in the district to hire full-time coaches. And as soon as there were coaches in place, Marie reworked the school schedule to provide time for weekly collaboration for grade-level teams. Marie is a school leader who never settles, and with coaches like Pam on her team, she has developed the systems to move their students toward success. With a population of 63.7% free and reduced lunch, Valhalla has consistently outperformed most schools with similar demographics. Their students regularly score over 70% in reading, writing, and math on the Washington state assessment (WASL). At Valhalla, being a data-driven school is paying off for both the students and teachers.

Meanwhile . . . in the Principal's Office

Principals, like teachers, are inundated with data. As the school leader, they often face the question of how to engage teachers in data in meaningful ways. They can't possibly have a conversation about every piece of data that crosses their desks, but they also can't keep the data to themselves. In an article titled "The Collaborative Advantage," Steele and Boudett (2009) write, "When school leaders face time pressure to improve achievement, they may be tempted to analyze data themselves and respond with instructional directives. Collaborative data use, admittedly, takes longer and requires hard work" (p. 58). Here are some ways for principals to lead teachers to engage in data.

Make Time for Conversations About Data

Data-rich conversations can't be rushed, and lack of time is almost always a barrier to data use (Ingram, Louis, & Schroeder, 2004; Marsh, Pane, & Hamilton, 2006). In order to provide teachers with regularly scheduled times within the work day to come together around data, principals create a master schedule that prioritizes teacher collaboration. Teachers are given the time to think deeply and collaboratively about student achievement in relationship to the standards and assessment data.

Participate in Conversations About Data and Hold Others Accountable to Do So as Well

Principals who value the process, participate in the process. They not only gain insight regarding where the teachers and students are and where they need to be, but are able to hold teachers accountable to take the necessary steps for increasing student achievement. Missing these conversations creates a blind spot for principals and makes it more difficult to set clear expectations for teachers.

Sometimes principals are tentative to join these conversations because they worry about how their presence will impact the group. This becomes less of an issue when there is a clear and well-understood process that is owned by the team of teachers. It can be a problem, however, if teachers are fumbling around and don't know the purpose or process for their time together. They may feel less than comfortable and may turn to the principal to take ownership. This speaks to the importance of developing self-sustaining groups that understand the purpose and know how to manage a productive conversation about the data. Let's face it, most principals are too busy to lead the process with every team in a school, and developing this capacity among coaches and teachers is essential.

Craft a Culture of Trust and Collaboration

Chapter 3 addresses the importance of crafting a school culture that is rich in trust and collaboration. This is particularly important for schools that choose to use data to drive their decision making, as data can either spur on meaningful dialogue about teaching and learning or breed suspicion and fear. By crafting a culture of trust and collaboration, the principal ensures that data moves the learning forward.

Tools and Techniques

Protocols for Using Data

With so much data and so little time, finding a process for diving into data is often the first step. The following protocols add structure to conversations about data.

Figure 4.8   Protocol for Analyzing Student Work

Purpose: This protocol is used to assist a group of teachers to reflectively analyze student work. It is used with teams of approximately four to six people. (Suggested time: 30–40 minutes)

Process:

1. The facilitator frames the purpose for the conversation and introduces the data/ student work that will be used.

2. In pairs, the group examines the data / student work with the following questions in mind: "What can we learn from the student work? What evidence can we tease out that indicates successes or breakdowns in student learning?

3. Each of the pairs shares in a whip-around, and they are as specific as possible. During this process, the facilitator charts the information that is shared.

4. The whole group discusses the implications for the teaching and learning based on what was noticed in the student work. Participants share in a whip-around, and at the end of the round the facilitator synthesizes new thinking.

5. Individually, each group member reflects in writing to name their next steps for instruction. The whole group shares their next steps, and the facilitator takes notes for follow-up.

Figure 4.9   Data Analysis Protocol to Determine a Schoolwide Focus

Purpose: This protocol is used to examine data in order to make decisions about how to tailor professional development and collaborative work to directly impact student learning. It is used with teams of teachers or a full faculty. (Suggested time: 90–100 minutes and can span a series of sessions)

Process:

1. The facilitator frames the purpose for the conversation and walks the group through the protocol and data that will be used. Data is organized into a user-friendly format and can include assessment data or samples of student work. (Approx. 5–10 minutes)

2. The group examines the data with the following question in mind: "What does the data show is a common need among our student population?" Participants respond in a whip-around, being as specific as possible. During this process, the facilitator charts the information that is shared. (Approx. 20 minutes)

3. The group collectively discusses what the implications are for their own teaching and learning based on what they noticed in the data. Participants share in a whip-around. At the end of the round, the facilitator synthesizes the themes from the discussion. (Approx. 20 minutes)

4. The group works to find agreement on a collective goal for students using the following guiding question: "What does it make sense for us to focus on in order to directly impact student learning?" At the end of the round, the facilitator names one area of focus that has been agreed on by the group. If agreement hasn't been reached, then the facilitator allows the discussion to continue and may refer the group back to the data for further analysis. The group does not move on to the next step until an agreement has been reached. (Approx. 15 minutes)

5. The group determines how to assess the impact of their work using the following guiding questions: "How will we measure the impact of this work? What assessments will we use to determine if and how we are meeting students' needs?" The facilitator charts the ideas that are presented by the group members. (Approx. 15 minutes)

6. Participants create a plan that includes next steps for the work. (Approx. 10 minutes)

7. The facilitator closes the conversation by clearly naming the focus, next steps, and assessment plan for the work. (Approx. 5 minutes)

Figure 4.10　Protocol for Assessment Wall Discussions

Purpose: This protocol is used to guide a team of teachers through a conversation using the assessment wall. It is used in teams of four to eight people. (Suggested time: 45 minutes)

Process:

1. Begin by moving students' names to match where they are based on the most recent assessments (reading, math, English-language development).

2. Identify students that are showing growth. Discuss possible factors that may be leading to this growth, paying particular attention to factors such as interventions, instructional strategies, etc.

3. Revisit which of these students may be receiving additional support or interventions and may no longer need these services. Discuss how these students will continue to be monitored if a change is made.

4. Identify students that are falling behind in their growth. Discuss possible factors, such as language acquisition, attendance, IEP goals, instruction not being focused enough, teacher unsure of next steps for child, etc.

5. Create a short-term plan for the students that are not meeting the standard or are falling behind in their growth. This may include a coaching cycle, informal coaching, different intervention strategies, more intensive support during class time, reaching out to the child's family, or professional development to target the identified need. Discuss how these students will continue to be monitored.

6. Discuss any trends that are surfacing as needs across the school. The principal, coach, and other support personnel arrange to follow up to develop a plan for how to provide support in these areas.

A Final Thought

Data is at the center of student-centered coaching. By emphasizing student evidence as the key element of teacher decision making, both DSST and Valhalla are seeing gains among students that defy their demographics. These are enormous dividends that help schools move beyond a position of fearing data that hits us after the fact or fails to inform our practice. Instead, we are in control as we get out ahead of the data to guide our decision making as teachers, coaches, and school leaders.

5

Measuring the Impact of Student-Centered Coaching

Inevitably, any conversation about coaching is followed by the question of how to evaluate it. Educators, from teachers to super-intendents, are wondering how we will know if putting coaches in our schools was worth the time and effort.

After numerous conversations with educators in the field of research and evaluation, I quickly realized that there are many unanswered questions when it comes to evaluating the impact of professional development and coaching. Educators are clamoring for a way to collect evaluation data that proves how coaching positively impacts students, yet a large group of researchers believe we can only indirectly measure the impact of coaching on student learning. Couple this with the times in which we find ourselves—with increasing pressures to demonstrate the efficacy of every penny we are spending in our schools—and it becomes clear that we can't settle for measuring only indirectly whether coaching has made an impact. We have to know for sure.

A Model for Evaluating Coaching

Killion is in agreement regarding the importance of measuring the impact of professional development and writes (2008),

Too many staff development efforts are still focused on select-
ing and implementing interventions rather than achieving
specific results. The mental model we hold about our work as
staff developers may block us from taking a results-oriented
approach. For too long, we have judged our own work by
standards such as the number of participants who enjoyed a
program or participated, degree of diversity of programs or
courses available, or creative uses of time. Regardless of our
rhetoric, as long as these are our standards, we have not, in
fact, adopted results for students as our highest goal. (p. 2)

I have always believed we could find a way to link coaching with
student achievement. Yet as a coach, I experienced mandates where I
was required to log my daily conversations, turn in my schedule, survey teachers, and keep track of which teachers participated in professional development. What I discovered was these forms of data
helped me track how I was spending my time, discover whether any
teachers were falling through the cracks, and stay organized, but they
didn't directly connect my work to student learning. I realized that if
we wanted to collect data that measured the impact of coaching on
students, then we had to collect a different kind of data. But what?

The question of evaluating coaching became more important while I
was working with a group of coaches in the St. Joseph School District in
Missouri. Their school board wanted proof that coaching was making a
difference with students—a fair request given the fact that the district had
invested a significant amount of resources to hire eighteen instructional
coaches across their elementary, middle, and high schools. I decided not to
settle for the argument that we can't link coaching with student achievement and went about creating a system that would help the coaches in
St. Joseph capture the data they needed to measure their impact.

When I began thinking about how to develop an evaluation system,
I was sensitive to the fact that the coaches in St. Joseph had their hands
full. I didn't want to add to their workload, but instead, whatever I came
up with had to reinforce their coaching practice and fit seamlessly into
their daily work with teachers and students. I also wanted to be sure that
something empirical came from the data so that we could present the
school board with the "hard data" they were requesting.

Many of the pieces were already in place in St. Joseph. The coaches
had been carefully selected based on their knowledge and skills. I had
worked with them on an ongoing basis to help them get their one-on-
one coaching up and running. And most were implementing coaching
cycles in their schools. Though some worked in two schools, they had
dedicated coaching jobs that provided them with a good amount of
time with teachers. Whatever evaluation system we chose had to tap

into what existed, so I bookended the basic structure of the coaching cycle with pre- and postassessments to come up with the following model for capturing data across a coaching cycle (Figure 5.1).

Figure 5.1   Capturing Data Across a Coaching Cycle

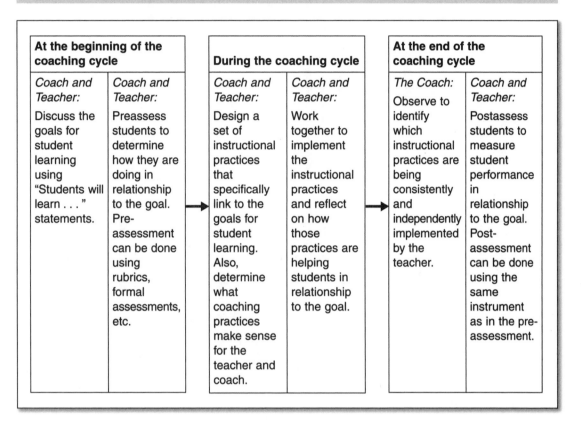

At the beginning of the coaching cycle		During the coaching cycle		At the end of the coaching cycle	
Coach and Teacher:	*Coach and Teacher:*	*Coach and Teacher:*	*Coach and Teacher:*	*The Coach:*	*Coach and Teacher:*
Discuss the goals for student learning using "Students will learn . . ." statements.	Preassess students to determine how they are doing in relationship to the goal. Pre-assessment can be done using rubrics, formal assessments, etc.	Design a set of instructional practices that specifically link to the goals for student learning. Also, determine what coaching practices make sense for the teacher and coach.	Work together to implement the instructional practices and reflect on how those practices are helping students in relationship to the goal.	Observe to identify which instructional practices are being consistently and independently implemented by the teacher.	Postassess students to measure student performance in relationship to the goal. Post-assessment can be done using the same instrument as in the pre-assessment.

When I presented this model to the coaches, they reacted just as I'd hoped . . . they raised the roof with choruses of, "This is what I've needed all along! Why didn't you bring this to us sooner?" They felt it reinforced the types of conversations they were having with teachers and provided a natural flow and rhythm that they could repeat again and again. Rather than becoming a distraction to their work, they recognized how it would help scaffold their development as coaches. They could see themselves having these conversations with teachers, and confessed that they had been feeling their way through most of their coaching conversations and weren't sure how their work was affecting the students.

Our next step was to make the evaluation process more concrete and help the coaches implement it as a natural addition to their coaching cycles. We recognized the need for a concrete tool and crafted the Results-Based Coaching Tool as a place for coaches to capture the data as they went (Figure 5.2).

Figure 5.2 Results-Based Coaching Tool

Teacher's Name:	Coach's Name:	
Coaching Cycle Focus:	**Dates of Coaching Cycle:** _____ to _____	
	beginning date	ending date

What is the student learning goal for this coaching cycle? What data is this goal based on?	*What instructional practices were determined by the coach and teacher to most likely produce the desired student learning goal?*	*What coaching practices were implemented during this coaching cycle? (check all that apply)*	*As a result of the coaching cycle, what instructional practices is the teacher now using on a consistent basis?*	*What is the evidence that students accomplished the desired learning goal?*
Student Learning Goal: Standard: **Baseline Data:** ____ % of students were able to do ____ as determined by the ____ assessment. Number of Students ____		☐ Demonstration teaching with a prebrief, lesson, and debrief ☐ Co-teaching with a prebrief, lesson, and debrief ☐ Collaborative planning ☐ Analysis of student work ☐ Teacher observation with a prebrief, lesson, and debrief ☐ Study group to discuss professional text that aligns to the student learning goal ☐ Other: ____		**Postassessment Data:** ____ % of students were able to do ____ as determined by the ____ assessment.

Using the Results-Based Coaching Tool:
At the Beginning of the Coaching Cycle

The coaches in St. Joseph were introduced to the Results-Based Coaching Tool (RBT) and were asked to try it out in a coaching cycle. Angie, a middle school instructional coach, decided she'd begin using it with Paula, a seventh-grade language arts teacher (Figure 5.3). Paula had indicated an interest in participating in a coaching cycle and was open to the idea.

The first step would be to focus the coaching cycle on a specific goal for students, so Angie began their first planning session with the simple question, "What are you noticing about your students and their writing?" Paula lamented, "I've definitely noticed that my students, especially my third-hour kids, aren't transferring what they have learned about conventions to their daily writing. Their writing is full of errors that shouldn't be there." While listening to Paula, Angie was thinking, "I suppose this could be a place to start," and suggested, "Well, I know it isn't very glamorous, but why not focus the coaching cycle on writing conventions, especially if that's what your students need?" They agreed to start there and hoped that by focusing on conventions now, they would be in a better position to move on to more sophisticated elements of writing instruction at a later date.

With the focus for the coaching cycle established, Angie inquired about whether Paula had any ideas for how they could collect some baseline data to further identify how the students were doing. Then they would be able to design instruction that would directly target their needs. Paula suggested a rubric from the Write Traits program because she had used it in the past and thought it was a good match. Angie agreed and suggested, "How about if we give the students a prompted writing assignment, it could really be about anything, and then assess the papers together the next time we meet. Then we'll be able to plan some instruction. Maybe we should do it with your third-hour kids since they are the ones that you are most concerned about." Paula liked the idea and agreed to bring the assessments to her next planning session with Angie.

They met a week later and Paula had the student writing in hand. She hadn't graded the assignments yet, so they scored them one by one and Angie added the following data to the Results-Based Coaching Tool.

- 0/22 students or 0% exceeded the standard for conventions
- 0/22 students or 0% were experienced
- 6/22 students or 26% were competent
- 13/22 students or 57% were developing

Figure 5.3 Results-Based Coaching Tool from Angie and Paula's Coaching Cycle

Teacher's Name: Paula		Coach's Name: Angie		
Coaching Cycle Focus: Student awareness and usage of conventions in their writing.		**Dates of Coaching Cycle:** September 26–November 11		
What is the student learning goal for this coaching cycle? What data is this goal based on?	*What instructional practices were determined by the coach and teacher to most likely produce the desired student learning goal?*	*What coaching practices were implemented during this coaching cycle? (check all that apply)*	*As a result of the coaching cycle, what instructional practices is the teacher now using on a consistent basis?*	*What is the evidence that students accomplished the desired learning goal?*
Student Learning Goal: Students will learn to use the basic conventions of writing within their written assignments.	• Focused mini-lessons on areas of concern and that tie to the standards for this grade level	☐ Analysis of student work	1. Analyze student work to select focus areas	**Postassessment Data:** Third hour (November 3) Write Trait Conventions Rubric
		☐ Weekly planning time with coach		6- 6/22– 27% (WOW)
Baseline Data: Third hour (October 4) Write Trait Conventions Rubric	• Active student involvement in mini-lessons through the use of highlighters	☐ Demonstration teaching with a prebrief, lesson, and debrief	2. Collaborative planning with other teachers to share ideas	5- 7/22– 32% (Experienced) 4- 8/22– 36% (Competent) 3- 1/22– 5% (Developing)
6- 0/23– 0% (WOW) 5- 0/23– 0% (Experienced) 4- 6/23– 26% (Competent)	• Connected mini-lessons to students' own writing	☐ Collaborative planning with team	3. Focused mini-lessons to teach conventions	2- 0/22– 0% (Emerging) 1- 0/22– 0% (Not Yet)
3- 13/23– 57% (Developing) 2- 3/23– 13% (Emerging) 1- 0/23– 0% (Not Yet)		☐ Teacher observation with a prebrief, lesson, and debrief	4. Immediate connection of mini-lesson to student writing	59% of students earned at least 5 points on the rubric.
0% of students earned at least 5 points on the rubric.			5. Observation of other teachers	5% of students earned 3 points or less on the rubric.
70% of students earned 3 points or less on the rubric.				

- 3/22 students or 13% were emerging
- 0/22 students or 0% were below emerging

The students' scores validated Paula's concerns and reinforced the focus they had chosen for their work together. The fact that 70% of the students were below standard made Paula grateful that she had enlisted help from Angie, and Angie was relieved that they had a clear plan for their work together.

Creating Assessment Checklists and Rubrics

We don't need to limit ourselves to a single assessment for every situation, but instead we can be creative in figuring out how we can best assess student learning. Angie and Paula had an assessment right at their fingertips that closely aligned with their goal for student learning. In other situations, the teacher and coach may craft an assessment to capture the data they are looking for. The key is to have the goal for student learning identified before the assessment tool is selected. Otherwise, the assessment tool may shift the coaching toward a goal that may not match the teachers' expectations for the students and could derail the coaching cycle. DuFour and Eaker write,

> The critical point to remember is that relying on any one model would be a seriously flawed assessment strategy. Assessment of a student's work should provide a rich array of information on his or her progress and achievement. Only multiple assessment procedures can offer such information. The challenge is to match appropriate assessment strategies to curricular goals and instructional methodologies. (1998, p. 172)

Creating your own assessment checklist or rubric makes sense if you don't have an assessment tool that matches your goal for student learning. An example of this is a coaching cycle I had with Margie that was focused on developing character in short stories. When we began our work together, Margie and I had an inkling of what good character development consisted of, but we needed to know more so we did some research using curriculum guides and web searches and came up with the following criteria for effective character development:

- The characters' inner feelings are described in a way that shows how their feelings and actions change across the story (dynamic vs. static).

- The characters' motivations are well described.
- The writer describes the main character's relationships with secondary characters.
- Dialogue is used in a way that helps the reader better understand the characters. Dialect and cultural prospective may be used.
- Characters seem "real"—based in real life.

Our checklist ended up driving the coaching cycle. It served as an assessment tool and also presented us with endless possibilities for instruction. We pulled it out each time we met and spent most of our conversations thinking about what instructional practices and materials would help students develop as writers. At the beginning of the coaching cycle, the students' characterization was mostly a simple description of physical appearance, and at the end it evolved into a rich array of writing techniques that directly matched the assessment checklist. By focusing on a goal for student learning and unpacking the skills that were involved, we were able to target the instruction and capture the impact on students.

Using the Results-Based Coaching Tool: During the Coaching Cycle

Angie and Paula are ready to do the fun part—design the instruction. This kicked off the second phase of the Results-Based Coaching Tool, or determining the instructional practices that make sense in relationship to the goal for student learning.

In the past, designing the instruction was where most coaching would begin. The coach and teacher would create terrific lessons, teach them, and reflect on them. What we found is without a goal for student learning and some baseline data, the coaching ended up being a collection of lessons and the impact was hard to measure. By backing up and naming the goal for student learning *first*, collecting assessment data *second*, and then designing the instruction, coaching becomes data driven and easier to measure.

When they began discussing lesson ideas, Paula confessed that she felt as though she had tried everything she could think of and needed some fresh ideas. Angie had spent time in her classroom and had noticed a lack of student engagement. She suggested they try some instructional practices that would address conventions in a way that would also get the students engaged. They decided to do this through shorter and more focused mini-lessons to target the conventions they wanted to see in student writing, using highlighters to engage students in revision strategies, and connecting the mini-lessons to the students' own writing so they could see where they were making mistakes.

Paula liked the idea but wasn't sure how to do this with her students, and Angie assured her that they would do this work side by side using the Gradual Release of Responsibility Model (Figure 5.4). When the coaching cycle was complete, Paula would be able to do it on her own.

To do this, Angie organized her work with Paula into the three stages found on the Gradual Release of Responsibility Model. First, they planned a few days' worth of mini-lessons that Angie modeled while Paula observed and took notes. At the end of each week, they reflected on the student work and instruction to decide what to do next. The second stage came a few weeks into the cycle with Paula planning and co-teaching alongside Angie. Some teachers I've worked with have hesitated to take this step, and I end up modeling instruction for far too long. What I've found is it helps to set the

Figure 5.4 Gradual Release of Responsibility Model

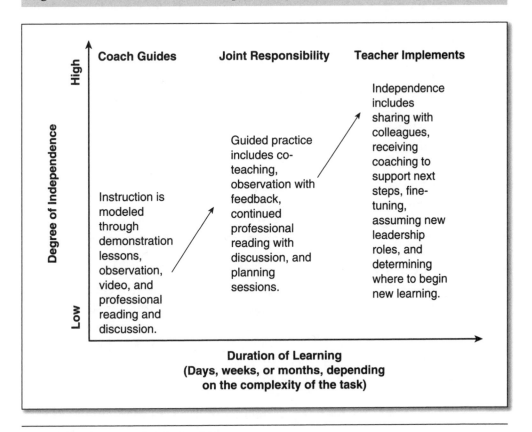

Adapted from Pearson and Gallagher, 1983.

expectation as early as possible that this is a part of the coaching cycle, just as Angie did with Paula. With time, they shifted to Paula doing most of the teaching on her own, just as Angie had promised. It's important to note that not all coaching cycles flow through the gradual release of responsibility in the same way. Some involve mostly co-teaching. Others emphasize a lot of modeling at first and then the teacher takes over. It really depends on the comfort level of the teacher as well as the teacher and coach relationship.

How well Angie and Paula collaborated together didn't happen by chance. It was carefully designed to ensure that their roles were clearly articulated. At the onset of the coaching cycle, Angie and Paula used the Teacher/Coach Agreement (Figure 5.5) to formalize

Figure 5.5 Teacher/Coach Agreement

Section 1: Coaching Focus

1. What do you hope students will learn as a result of our coaching work?
2. Is there any student work or data that could help us decide on a focus that would make the most impact with students?

Section 2: Strategies for Coaching and Collaboration

3. How would you like to interact during our time in the classroom (co-teach, model, observe)?
4. I suggest a weekly planning session for 30–45 minutes; what time works for you?
5. It is also important for me to be in your classroom for one to three times per week; what time is best for you based on your goal for students?
6. How would you like to communicate between our planning sessions (meetings, e-mails, other)?

Section 3: Meeting the Teacher's Needs

7. Do you have any other concerns about the coaching?
8. Is there anything you want me to be sure to do as your coach?

the details of their collaboration. The Teacher/Coach Agreement helps a teacher and coach begin their relationship in a clear and open way by encouraging dialogue about areas that could foster assumptions about roles and may even create conflict. In their book *Taking the Lead: New Roles for Teachers and School-Based Coaches,* Joellen Killion and Margie Harrison (2006) advocate for explicit conversations about roles and responsibilities and write,

> Forming partnership agreements is a fundamental skill coaches depend on in their work almost daily. Like savvy, external consultants, coaches work closely with those whom

they serve to identify their responsibilities, processes, and outcomes of their work. The intention is to create a degree of intimacy between the client and the coach that allows them to work together more openly and honestly. (p. 119)

Using the Results-Based Coaching Tool: At the End of the Coaching Cycle

At the end of a seven-week coaching cycle, Paula and Angie assessed the student learning using the same Write Source rubric they had used to collect baseline data. They found that 95% of the students were at competent or above compared with 26% when they began their work together, which gave them a lot to celebrate.

- 6/22 students or 27% exceeded the standard for conventions
- 7/22 students or 32% were experienced
- 8/22 students or 36% were competent
- 1/22 students or 5% were developing
- 0/22 students or 0% were emerging
- 0/22 students or 0% were below emerging

Their coaching cycle was coming to a close, and thanks to such a great impact, Paula was committed to using the practices she and Angie had implemented: focused mini-lessons on areas of concern and that tie to the standards for this grade level, active student involvement in mini-lessons through the use of highlighters, and connecting mini-lessons to the students' own writing. Angie wanted to collect some evidence about how Paula was doing with these instructional practices, so with her permission, Angie observed in a few of Paula's other classes to document the teaching practices that she was using on her own. This helped Angie gather evidence about the change in teacher practice as a result of the coaching cycle, which is another important piece of information to measure the coach's impact. And sure enough, Paula was implementing the practices on her own throughout the day.

Since it was her first time using the Results-Based Coaching Tool, Angie wanted to know what Paula thought and scheduled an exit interview to discuss postassessment data, engage in goal setting for the future, and reflect on which of the coaching practices were the most helpful. With this information, Angie would be better prepared to work with Paula (and other teachers) in the future. Sample questions for exit interviews include the following (Figure 5.6).

Figure 5.6 Sample Questions for Exit Interviews

- How did you benefit from the coaching cycle?
- How did your students benefit from the coaching cycle?
- What did the assessment data reveal at the end of the coaching cycle?
- If you didn't see any benefit, how can we adjust the coaching?
- Which of the coaching practices were most useful / least useful to you?
- What is a future goal for student learning?
- What is a future goal for your learning?
- Would you like to participate in another coaching cycle? If so, when?
- What other feedback or questions do you have?

Evaluating the Impact of Coaching Small Groups of Teachers

Any coach will tell you that effective coaching doesn't only take place with individual teachers; it also occurs with small groups. Small-group coaching cycles include groups of three to six teachers and consist of the following stages (Figure 5.7).

Figure 5.7 Small-Group Coaching Cycles

1. Determine a purpose for the group work that ties directly to student learning
   - What is the goal for student learning?
   - How does the goal connect with our school improvement plan?
2. Learn from the student evidence
   - What student work samples will inform our thinking?
   - How will we analyze and discuss the student work?
   - What can we learn when we analyze the student work?
   - What is our *specific* student learning goal?
3. Extend the group's learning
   - What new learning does our group need to commit to?
   - What can we study (books, chapters, video, observation) to extend our thinking?
4. Design the instructional plan
   - How will our teaching look the same or different now that we've analyzed the student evidence?
   - What will we do next as teachers?
   - What lessons will we design?
5. Revisit student work to measure student growth
   - What was the impact of our work on the students?
   - What did revisiting the student work teach us?

Measuring the impact of small-group coaching cycles is similar to individual coaching cycles and uses a Results-Based Coaching Tool that has been designed for this purpose (Figure 5.8).

Figure 5.8 Results-Based Coaching Tool for Small Groups

Teachers' Names:		Coach's Name:	
Purpose for the Group Work:		**Dates of Small Group Coaching Cycle:**	
What did we learn from analyzing the student work?	*What is our goal for student learning?*	*How will we extend our learning as a group?*	*As a result of the small = group coaching cycle, what instructional practices are the teachers planning to use?*	*What is the evidence that students accomplished the desired learning goal?*
What student work did we examine? **What did we find?** **Preassessment Data:**	**Student Learning Goal:**	Text-Based Collaboration Problem-Based Collaboration Observation: Demonstration Observation: Peer-Based Video One-On-One Coaching More examination of student work Other:		**Postassessment Data:**

97

Julie is working with a team of middle school teachers who have asked for her help with teaching persuasive essays—something that they know will be assessed later in the year. At the beginning of the coaching cycle, Julie suggests they examine the persuasive essays the students have already written to collect baseline data. Samantha—a new teacher—looks unsure and says, "Guys, I'm not sure I know enough about what persuasive writing looks like to assess anything." The others nod in agreement and Scott adds, "I've been teaching persuasive writing for years, but to be honest, it's not something I've ever really studied. I wouldn't know how to assess it beyond some basic traits." Julie appreciates their honesty and sees this as an opportunity for some shared learning as a team. She suggests, "How about if we read and discuss some published persuasive writing and then we can develop the assessment checklist based on what we see? I'll even volunteer to collect some samples for next week's meeting."

The following week they read and discuss a collection of pieces written by authors like Leonard Pitts from the *Miami Herald* and Steve Lopez from the *Los Angeles Times*. They also analyze a rubric for persuasive writing that Scott found online. In their analysis, they notice that the pieces with the best argument provide both a pro and counterargument within the piece. Upon discovering this, Amy says, "I feel that if the students don't address the counterargument, then their writing misses an opportunity. For instance, if a student was trying to persuade a school to purchase a laptop for every student. Then wouldn't he have to address counterarguments like the expense or issues around safety and the Internet? I mean, you can't just argue that everyone should have one and not make these points, can you?" They agree and decide to make providing a pro and counterargument their focus.

Now they are ready to collect some baseline data. They assign the students to write a short, persuasive piece about any subject. When they come back together to see what the students did, they find that 27% of the students addressed the counterargument in their pieces. This confirms their plan for helping students master this skill and this becomes the focus of their work together. They collaborate for the next month in the small-group coaching cycle and through the use of mentor texts (some that came directly from their earlier study), graphic organizers, and carefully designed lessons, their students demonstrate a clear understanding of how to include a pro and con argument within a persuasive piece of writing. In fact, the baseline data demonstrated movement from 27% to 87% on the postassessment.

Throughout the small-group coaching cycle, Julie charts the group's progress so that at the end they had something to celebrate . . . something that wouldn't have happened if Julie hadn't paid close attention to measuring student learning in relationship to their collaborative work (Figure 5.9).

Figure 5.9 Results-Based Coaching Tool for Small Groups From Julie's Team

Teachers' Names: Samantha, Scott, Amy		**Coach's Name:** Julie S.	
Purpose for the Group Work: Unit of Study: Persuasion		**Dates of Small Group Coaching Cycle:** October 1 to November 27	
What did we learn from analyzing the student work?	*What is our goal for student learning?*	*How will we extend our learning as a group?*	*As a result of the small-group coaching cycle, what instructional practices are the teachers planning to use?*	*What is the evidence that students accomplished the desired learning goal?*
What student work did we examine? Persuasive pieces that students did unassisted at the beginning of the unit. **What did we find?** When we looked at the work, we noticed that the students were able to give the pro argument with a series of examples with no attention to the counter-argument. **Preassessment Data:** 24% of students were able to directly address the counter-argument as determined by the rubric for persuasive writing.	**Student Learning Goal:** Students will give a pro and con argument within their persuasive essays. They will directly address the counter-argument as part of their thesis.	X Text-Based Collaboration Problem-Based Collaboration Observation: Demonstration X Observation: Peer-Based Video X One-On-One Coaching X More examination of student work X Other: look for and share a set of mentor texts to teach this writing skill	1. Find and use mentor texts that do this well. Use the mentor text to show students how much more powerful persuasive essays are when they address the counter-argument. 2. Develop a graphic organizer (maybe a T chart) that would help the students examine both sides before doing the writing. 3. Work with students on how to organize the pieces to include a pro and con argument—develop this through mentor text.	**Postassessment Data:** 87% of students were able to directly address the counter-argument as determined by the rubric for persuasive writing.

Meanwhile . . . in the Principal's Office

The idea of measuring progress clearly appeals to principals. Yet many principals have experienced the tension that flares up the minute they bring up the subject of evaluating the impact of coaching. Nothing makes a coach more nervous than being asked, "What impact have you made with students and teachers?" This tension has led us to shy away from asking this important question and has given coaching the image of lacking in accountability and results. Here's what principals can do to change that.

Establish a Transparent System of Evaluation

Establishing a clear and transparent process for collecting evidence across individual and small-group coaching cycles creates the expectation that student evidence will be a part of every conversation. Tools like the Results-Based Coaching Tool become familiar and expected, adding a greater degree of rigor to coaching while also providing data about its impact.

Keep Student Learning at the Forefront of Every Conversation

When student learning is at the center of every conversation, it becomes far more natural to use that student work to measure the impact of coaching and professional development. The tools that have been shared in this chapter depend on looking at student work and asking questions like, "What are our goals for student learning and how will these practices get us there?" By setting the tone that this is what is expected in the school, the principal takes an important step in leading coaching to make a greater impact across the school.

Observe for the Instructional Practices That are Taking Shape

The last phase of the Results-Based Coaching Tool is a reporting of the instructional practices that are being used independently by the teacher. When teachers are close to finishing a coaching cycle, spend time in the classroom to observe the practices that are taking shape as a result of the coaching cycle. This reinforces the teachers' participation in coaching and provides invaluable insight to how the teachers' pedagogical knowledge has evolved.

Provide Opportunities to Share and Celebrate New Learning

One of the best ways to sell a product is to share all the ways it makes a difference to the consumer. The same is true for coaching. By providing opportunities to celebrate new learning among teachers and students, the principal continues to motivate teachers to tap into this valuable commodity.

Tools and Techniques

With all that happens in a coach's day, it is crucial to organize our activities, thoughts, resources, and materials. I've tried using a binder with a tab for each teacher. I've tried cute little notebooks. I've tried keeping all of my notes on a laptop. And what I've learned is no single system works for every coach or for every situation. In addition to the Results-Based Coaching Tool, the following logs fit a variety of purposes for gathering specific types of information to measure the impact of coaching.

Coaching Logs

It may be my age, or the nature of coaching, but if I don't write it down, I forget it. By chronicling the work I do with individual teachers, I am able to recognize growth across time and identify places for future growth. Typically, I share what I've written in my coaching logs (Figure 5.10) only with the teacher, unless the district requires they be collected for evaluation purposes.

Teacher Participation Logs

Collecting data about teacher participation is vital if a district is interested in evaluating the impact of coaching. This information allows a district to compare the degree to which a teacher participates in professional development against student achievement. Since not all forms of professional development make the same impact, the following log includes a scale for each professional development activity, such as one-on-one coaching, professional learning communities, study groups, observations, and professional development sessions (Figure 5.11).

Figure 5.10   Coaching Log

Teacher Name:

Coach Name:

Date:

1. What is our focus for student learning?

2. What did we discuss today?

3. What did we do in the classroom today?

4. What are students doing as a result of our work together?

5. What are our next steps?

Teacher's Next Steps:

Coach's Next Steps:

Figure 5.11   Teacher Participation Log

Professional Development Scale

3-Day Fall Institute = 3 points
1-Day District Workshop = 1 point
One-On-One Coaching Cycle = 4 points
Small-Group Coaching Cycle = 3 points
Informal Planning with a Coach = 2 points
1-Day Classroom Observation = 3 points
Grade-Level Meetings = 2 points
Study Group = 2 points

Teacher Name	Activities	Dates	Focus	Total Points
Leah	3-Day Institute Grade-Level Meetings 1:1 Coaching Cycle	8/25–8/27 Weekly 10/10–11/30	Math Curriculum Math/Literacy Science Notebooks	9 points

A Final Thought

Understanding our impact serves to fundamentally motivate us to grow as professionals. We can't just think about measuring our impact to protect ourselves from the powers that be. We must look at evaluation as a way to capture and celebrate our successes. When it came time to report the impact of their coaching to the school board, the coaches in St. Joseph had the data to prove their efficacy with students. But even more important was the fact that they knew their work was making a difference. That alone makes it worth the effort.

Section III

Practices for Student-Centered Coaching

6

Student-Centered Classroom Observations

"I'm not sure it will help anyone to observe in my classroom . . . but I'm willing to do it," shrugs Nicole, a special education teacher in the Edmonds School District in Seattle, Washington. Nicole is a dedicated and earnest teacher of a challenging population of students with special needs. She has agreed to host an upcoming observation, or Student-Centered Learning Lab, while she teaches a group of nine third graders and two fourth graders who are on individualized education plans (IEP) and are pulled out to receive intensive math instruction.

Edmonds School District has spent four years creating a districtwide model for student-centered observations like the one that will be taking place in Nicole's classroom. As part of this project, Nicole has observed in other classrooms on a variety of occasions and knows that hosting a group of colleagues will provide her with invaluable insight about her students. She decides that she can't pass it up.

Three Generations of Learning Labs

Learning labs create a framework for teachers to get into each other's classrooms to learn alongside one another. In *Learning Along the Way* (Sweeney, 2003), I shared a process for learning labs in which teachers observe in model classrooms to develop their skills and reflect with colleagues. Since then, teacher observations have become increasingly more common and have evolved into the following formats.

The First Generation of Learning Labs—Model Classrooms

Learning labs were introduced in 1991 by staff developers Stephanie Harvey and Liz Stedem from the Public Education & Business Coalition (PEBC) in Denver, Colorado. Steph and Liz had just returned from observing in classrooms that were affiliated with Teachers College in New York. Part of their visit included an observation in Judy Davis's classroom, where they were struck by not only the quality of the teaching but also by the effect of the observation. They returned to Denver and designed the PEBC Lab Network in which teachers were provided with the opportunity to observe and reflect on high-quality instruction in a network of model classrooms.

In the early to mid-1990s, instructional practice was going through a dramatic shift toward a balanced approach that emphasized deep thinking, comprehension, and problem solving. These areas proved to be complex endeavors for teachers, and labs served an important need in that they helped teachers see what the instruction looked like so they could figure out how to implement such practices in their own classrooms. Observations in model classrooms were teacher centered and focused directly on how the host teacher was going about the business of teaching with the expectation that the observers would go back and implement it themselves. It was vitally important for the lab hosts to use current educational research in order to provide high-quality instruction to their students. Therefore, PEBC carefully vetted lab hosts in model classrooms to meet the following criteria:

- Participate in extensive professional development and coaching opportunities.
- Are thoughtful about teaching and learning.
- Demonstrate research-based teaching in a real classroom context.
- Have the confidence to host visitors.
- Are capable of discussing the purposes behind what they do with their students.
- Are authentic readers and writers.
- Set a positive tone in the classroom.
- Are passionate about teaching.

Once the model classroom teachers were determined, they hosted regular groups of visitors from other schools and districts. Some of the observations were multiday visits and others took place in a single day. Each observation was carefully planned, facilitated, and guided by the Protocol for Observing in a Model Classroom (see "Tools and Techniques" at the end of this chapter).

The Second Generation of Learning Labs—Peer Learning Labs

A few years later, a middle school principal in the Denver Public Schools approached PEBC about designing learning labs that would counteract a closed-door culture and extend teacher collaboration. He didn't see model classrooms as an option since he worried that they would further the divide among the teachers. PEBC coaches Anne Patterson and Brooke O'Drobinak helped develop peer learning labs that created the opportunity for teachers' work collaboratively to explore questions about how to improve their teaching with the goal of improving student learning.

Peer learning labs are hosted by any willing teacher on staff and emphasize the host teacher as a learner rather than as an expert. They are based on a focus question that is provided by the lab host, which shifts the observation toward thinking together about how to work through challenges related to teaching and learning rather than on sharing expertise. The Protocol for Peer Learning Labs is intrinsic to the process, as it provides a safe environment for both the observers and lab host to come together as learners (see "Tools and Techniques").

Since peer learning labs aren't based on expertise, the criteria for lab hosts is somewhat different than for teachers in model classrooms and includes teachers who

- are learners and are reflective about their practice;
- craft an authentic focus question;
- participate in school-based coaching; and
- are engaged members of the school community.

The Third Generation of Learning Labs— Student-Centered Learning Labs

Much like peer learning labs, student-centered labs revolve around a focus question that is generated by the lab host. However, in our experience, even with a focus question, much of the observers' attention was on what the teacher was or was not doing. Student-centered labs further focus the observation through a set of student indicators, or "look for's," shifting the focus onto student evidence while still allowing teachers to glean ideas from the classrooms in which they observe. In Edmonds, we progressed from model classrooms to peer learning labs, and we are now implementing student-centered labs because we found value in the fact that they focus more directly on the students.

Nicole has had this group of students for just a few weeks, and her current focus is teaching them how to use math journals in order to explain their mathematical reasoning. To help prepare for the observation, Nicole's coach and lab facilitator, Julia, meets with her to craft the focus question and look for's. They decide the focus question will be, "How does our use of writing help support our thinking and understanding in math?" They talk about some possible look for's and Nicole decides to think it over for a few days.

On the morning of the lab, the prebriefing session begins with Nicole explaining her student population and what she has been working on over the past few weeks. She has been using a math workshop that includes a mini-lesson, work period, and share session, and her current focus is on problem solving and using math vocabulary. She explains that she wants the students to be metacognitive when they are solving math problems and thinks that using math journals will help them capture their thinking, and that a secondary goal for her students is to be independent workers and risk takers.

The visitors include classroom teachers, a few elementary principals, and two district coaches. As Nicole shares her goals for the students, Julia charts the following look for's that will help keep the observation focused on the students:

- Students use their math journals
- Students' math journals include math vocabulary
- Students solve problems in two ways and then communicate which way works best
- Students' math journals show that they are using a system for checking their work
- Students demonstrate cognitive rigor and stamina
- Students work independently
- Students share with and learn from their peers

Julia wants to be sure that the observers understand their role while they are in Nicole's classroom and shares a set of norms for the observation. She also provides a note-taking sheet for capturing evidence as the group observes (see "Tools and Techniques"). To further anchor the observation, Julia will hang the chart of look for's in Nicole's classroom to remind the observers of their purpose and focus for the observation. But before heading there, Julia encourages the group to ask clarifying questions so they are well prepared for the observation.

We arrive in the classroom and get settled as the students open their math journals and waste no time turning their attention to Nicole. She begins with a warm-up on place value and carefully reminds the students to write the steps they took to solve each problem. She reminds them they need to solve problems in two ways and decide which is the best method. They discuss what it means to be metacognitive problem-solvers, and she provides them with the language of, "First, then, next, last" to use in their math journals.

The observers have been encouraged to sit directly behind the students so they are close enough to see and hear the thinking that students are doing in their journals and with their partners. As the students begin working in pairs to solve and write about a set of math problems, the observers collect a rich array of student evidence in their notes. At times, the observers glance to the chart of look for's and return to their notebooks to jot down more observations. The lesson wraps up, and I am interested to see what the group may have gained from observing in Nicole's classroom.

In the debriefing session, Julia reorients the group to the Protocol for Student-Centered Lab (Figure 6.1) and gives them a few minutes to read over their notes and think about what they would like to share. Nicole prepares herself to listen and take notes about what student evidence was collected by the group.

As they debrief the lesson, the observers detail specific things they saw students doing that related to Nicole's look for's, including the following:

- "I saw Tracy and Mayra write in their notebooks, 'First we did a proof drawing.'"
- "I noticed that the students are very used to using their math journals."
- "I heard students using math vocabulary when they worked with their partners."
- "I was struck by how the students were confident as they dug into a challenging math problem."
- "The students clearly were used to writing how they went about their thinking in math."
- "I noticed how the pieces of the math workshop allowed the students time to work together and think deeply about math."

Figure 6.1 Protocol for Student-Centered Learning Labs

Focus Question: How does our use of writing help support our thinking and understanding in math?	
Prebriefing Session to Frame the Observation (45 minutes)	• The host teacher introduces the group to the focus question in order to help the group understand both the teaching and student learning. The teacher shares recent lessons and how the students have responded. The teacher may also choose to share artifacts from the classroom such as charts, student work, or other assessment data. • While the teacher shares, the facilitator charts a set of "look for's" that will serve the group during the debriefing process using the following guiding question, "What will it look like if the students are demonstrating the intended learning?" • The facilitator reminds the group of the observation norms, and the group is invited to ask clarifying questions to the host teacher.
Observe the Teaching and Learning (50–60 minutes)	• The group observes the instruction. While observing, participants take notes that are specific to the focus question and look for's.

Debrief the Teaching and Learning (60 minutes)	• The group debriefs in the following rounds. Throughout each round, the facilitator ensures that the responses are specific and objective and do not include feedback or suggestions. Each round is done as a "whip-around" so that the discussion moves in an orderly fashion from one person to the next. Participants may pass when it is their turn to speak.
	
	o Round One: Student Evidence
	   What specific evidence can you provide to the teacher regarding the focus question and look for's?
	o Round Two: Implications
	   What are the broader implications of what you observed? What does this mean for your teaching and learning?
	o Round Three: Response From the Host Teacher
	   The teacher responds by thinking aloud about what was shared. How has the teacher's thinking changed? What is a future goal for instruction? How will student learning be assessed?
	o Round Four: Next Steps for Instruction
	   Each group member shares a next step for their instruction that evolved from the observation.

Due to the design of the protocol, each round takes the group deeper into the evidence and what it means for the students. Julia reminds the group that this is not the time to make suggestions about how Nicole could have done things differently, because why would anyone volunteer to host peer labs if they were going to be on the receiving end of what they "should have" or "could have" done? Instead, by framing a student-centered lab on collecting evidence around students, the focus stays both safe and rigorous for everyone who participates.

After hearing what the group observed, Nicole shares her thinking. She feels more confident that the students are applying the challenging concept of metacognition and is thrilled that they were working at such an independent level after just a few weeks of instruction. She decides that her next step will be to teach the students to write the sequence of their problem solving while also teasing out more of the mathematical thinking and vocabulary. She also thinks she will try to create some intermediate assessments where students write their solutions using the problem-solving skills and vocabulary that she has been emphasizing.

After hearing from Nicole, each of the observers shares his or her own thinking and next steps from the observation. They discuss their goals for their students and begin thinking about how they will assess the impact of what they choose to do. One of the principals is struck by the rigor in Nicole's classroom and plans to revisit how they are approaching special education. A third-grade teacher shares how he will introduce metacognition in his math class since he uses it already in reading and hadn't really thought how it applied to math. Others were excited to see how similar the math workshop structure is to their reader's and writer's workshops and wanted to get it up and running right away. A few teachers decide to meet right after to begin crafting a rubric for what it means to be metacognitive in math. No matter their individual roles, everyone walks away from the student-centered lab with their own meaning and next steps.

Which Type of Lab Is Right for You?

Student-centered and peer learning labs are open, inclusive, and accessible for all teachers. They serve an important role in building a collegial school culture in which teachers think and learn together. Model classrooms offer an enormous amount of support in districts that are initiating a new instructional program or curriculum because they provide teachers with opportunities to see what it looks like and then go back and do the same thing in their classrooms. They are also particularly useful in districts that have a large population of new teachers as they provide a large degree of scaffolding and support.

Student-centered and peer labs are designed at the school level and are typically managed and facilitated by a school-based coach. Designing a network of model classrooms is better done at the district level because naming model classrooms within a school site causes strain and competition that can damage relationships and school culture. Creating cross-school observations in model classrooms diffuses tension since teachers are out of their own school community for the observations. The following criteria will help you consider which type of learning lab is the best fit for your school or district:

Model classrooms are a good fit if you

- have a large number of new teachers;
- have identified classrooms and teachers that model exemplary instruction;
- are implementing a new program or curriculum;
- have district-level personnel to manage the project;
- are less concerned with building a collegial culture; and
- have district resources to provide teachers with the necessary release time.

Peer learning labs are a good fit if you

- are more concerned with building a collegial culture;
- have school-level personnel, such as a coach, to manage the project;
- feel that there is enough trust among teachers to get the project up and running (if not, building some basic level of collegiality might be a first step in the process); and
- have school or district resources to provide teachers with the necessary release time.

Student-centered labs are a good fit if you

- are interested in guiding teachers to use student evidence in their daily decision making;
- are interested in building a collegial school culture;
- have school-level personnel, such as a coach, to manage the project;
- feel that there is enough trust among teachers to get the project up and running (if not, building some basic level of collegiality might be a first step in the process); and
- have school or district resources to provide teachers with the necessary release time.

Coaching and Learning Labs

Coaching and learning labs are inherently linked. I was reminded of this when I observed a peer learning lab at a large, urban high school. I had heard great things about how the school was going about learning labs and I wanted to see it for myself. The lab was facilitated by the literacy coach, and the lab host was a language arts teacher who was working to engage his students by using poetry that had been written by Chicano poets. He was finding that his students were having a hard time connecting with the typical literature he had been assigning and wanted to see how they engaged when reading more gritty literature that reflected their background. The observing teachers included a math teacher, a drama teacher, and a social studies teacher. The group had a prebriefing session in which the hosting teacher explained his rationale for the lesson and asked his colleagues to collect evidence regarding how the students engaged with the text. Then they observed a 50-minute block of instruction that was followed by a 90-minute debriefing session. As I listened, I heard the teachers challenging one another to think deeply about the connection between the students and the text that we ask them to read. They then discussed the state assessment and wondered how we can prepare them to read text that may not be as personally relevant. Throughout the conversation, an array of profound, thought-provoking, and sometimes intimidating questions were raised and discussed by the teachers. At the end of the session, I asked the teachers what they thought about participating in these types of labs and what the benefits were for them and their students. One of the teachers turned to me and said, "I find these labs to be incredibly useful . . . in fact, I'd trade in every other type of professional development to just participate in these labs." I'm thinking, "Yes, they like the labs!" Then he went on, "But . . . I also find it to be incredibly frustrating when there isn't any follow-up. We come up with all of these great ideas and questions, and then nothing happens. We are left hanging." At that moment, I realized that I had made a significant mistake when it came to learning labs. I had been thinking of them as stand-alone professional development events, rather than as a part of a larger interwoven tapestry of professional development. Of course they felt like this; their school of over 1,500 students had one literacy coach who also had her own teaching responsibilities. Peer learning labs were taking place on a monthly basis with several teachers, and it was no wonder their coach was struggling to provide individualized follow-up support to each teacher. We had to do something!

The coach and I stayed late that afternoon and crafted a follow-up mechanism that pulled the teachers back together as a small group a month after the lab took place. During and following the labs, she enlisted teachers to participate in coaching cycles to help them see their ideas to fruition. She also tapped into their existing study groups as a venue to follow up on labs. Finally, with support from the principal, the coach worked to determine a shared focus for teacher learning that would connect the professional development activities that were taking place already. With these changes, the labs didn't feel disconnected but rather fit nicely into a comprehensive system of support for teachers.

Informal Observations That Make an Impact

Teachers crave the opportunity to get into one another's classroom, whether it is down the hall or down the street, and informal observations can forward the development of a reflective and collaborative school culture with less time and resources. In *Learning Along the Way*, I shared the story of Keith. A thoughtful first-grade teacher, Keith adopted the new districtwide curriculum with ease. He was a gentle teacher who worked hard to make sure the English-language learners in his classroom became fluent readers, writers, and speakers of English. In comparison, many other teachers in the district struggled to adopt the same curriculum with a similar population of students.

In no time, word got out about Keith's successes and teachers began flocking to his classroom to see how it looked. The observations were not part of a formal learning lab structure and the teachers usually came without the help of a facilitator, so Keith gracefully tried to teach *and* explain his thinking to the visiting teachers. He finally said, "Enough" when a teacher came into his classroom, watched him teach for 45 minutes, and left without even an introduction. Keith's story teaches us that informal observations can sometimes be too informal, and the following features are important to maintain their integrity and make an impact.

Creating a Purpose for Informal Observations

For observations to have meaning, both the host and observing teachers need to know what they are there to learn, think about, and implement in their own classrooms. A way to set a purpose for informal observations is for the host teacher to write a letter to observers that outlines what the teacher is working toward with students, what has been taught in the past, where the instruction is headed, information about the student population, and background on the teacher's beliefs about teaching. After reading such a letter, the observers will have a better sense of what they will be observing and can set their own purpose for the observation. Another way to set purpose is through a prebriefing conversation before the observation. In this conversation, a facilitator who is familiar with the host teacher briefs the group on what they will see and provides some ideas for things to take away from the experience and ways to connect what they will observe to their own contexts.

Ensuring a Skilled Facilitation

Rarely does it make sense to have teachers observe in classrooms without a facilitator or coach. A facilitator builds a bridge between the host and observers and helps prepare both for an observation that is respectful and rigorous. More often than not, the facilitator is a coach who knows the host teacher and is able to clarify and focus the observation. The facilitator also sets norms for the observing teachers and manages details like schedule and release times.

Creating Time for Reflection

The example of the nameless teacher observing Keith is a reminder that *all* observations need to include a time for reflection. It is not enough to observe in a classroom and then go our separate ways, because meaning is made through the conversation that follows. At the very least, the facilitator sets aside 20–30 minutes for the teachers to discuss the following:

- What did you observe among the students and teacher in the classroom?
- What are the implications for you as a teacher?
- What are you going to take back to your classroom?

Meanwhile . . . in the Principal's Office

Not all schools are ready for learning labs, and it is naïve to believe that learning labs are a good fit for schools that have toxic cultures or cultures that lack a degree of trust and openness, or schools that don't have the necessary resources such as a trained facilitator and time set aside for reflection. Without these key ingredients, classroom observations may reach a few teachers who come with a reflective disposition, but will not make a systematic difference in the school. Some options for developing a readiness for learning labs are the following:

- Help teachers become accustomed to collaborative work by creating ongoing conversations that focus on teacher practice and student learning
- Regularly use student work to guide collaborative conversations among teachers
- Include the principal in collaborative conversations to build a bridge of trust between the school leader and teachers
- If the district offers a network of model classrooms, engage teachers in these observations
- Train a facilitator, such as a coach or lead teacher, to manage the lab process

Measuring the Impact of Observations

While many principals see the inherent value of classroom observations, they also want to be sure that observations are an appropriate use of time and resources. Evaluating the impact of classroom observations involves capturing data based on short-term and long-term outcomes across the three areas of school climate, teaching practice, and student learning (Figure 6.2).

Figure 6.2   Measuring Short-Term and Long-Term Outcomes of Learning Labs

Short-Term Outcomes—data to be collected during or immediately following the learning lab

Climate/Collaboration

1. What did you find was the most meaningful aspect of the observation?
2. Would you participate again in this type of professional development? Why or why not?
3. How did it feel to interact with your colleagues in this way?
4. In what ways do you anticipate learning labs will impact your school climate? Why?

Teaching Practice

1. What changes to your teaching practice do you plan to make as a result of the observation? Why?
2. What support and resources will you need to make these changes?

Student Learning

1. What is a goal for student learning that has stemmed from the observation (i.e., My students will . . .)?
2. What are some steps you plan to take to achieve this goal?

Long-Term Outcomes—data to be collected three to four weeks following the learning lab

Climate/Collaboration

1. How has your work with colleagues evolved since the observation?

Teaching Practice

1. What changes are well established in your classroom and can be attributed to the observation?
2. What teaching artifacts can you share that represent changes you have made to your teaching as a result of the observation (i.e., classroom charts, assignments, rubrics, etc.)?

Student Learning

1. What growth have you identified among your students?
2. What data or student evidence have you collected that demonstrates increased student learning as a result of the observation?

Tools and Techniques

Protocols for Observations in Model Classrooms and Peer Learning Labs

There are a few key distinctions between the protocols for observations in model classrooms and peer learning labs. Since the lab hosts for model classrooms have been vetted, supported, and well prepared for the process, observers are encouraged to question and probe the host teacher. Such questioning is not a part of the peer learning lab process because the hosts are meant to be seen as peers who are openly sharing the challenges they face as teachers. Probing teachers in this type of lab could be interpreted as a threat or criticism and may compromise the process. For more detailed protocols for observations in model classrooms and peer learning labs, see Figures 6.3 and 6.4.

Figure 6.3   Protocol for Observations in Model Classrooms

Prebriefing Session (30 minutes)	• The lab host gives background and context for the work. The facilitator discusses norms for the observation and participants ask clarifying questions.
Observation (50–60 minutes)	• Observers take notes to share during the debriefing session.
Debriefing Session (60 minutes)	• The group debriefs in the following rounds: ○ Round 1: *What did you see?* The group describes what they saw during the observation in a nonjudgmental manner. This is done as a "whip-around" so that the discussion moves in an orderly fashion from one person to the next. Participants may pass when it is their turn to speak. The facilitator summarizes and/or charts the round, capturing important themes and ideas that emerged from the discussion. ○ Round 2: *What was the impact on student learning?* The facilitator focuses the round on how the teaching impacted student learning. This discussion is done as a whip-around so that each person has an opportunity to add a comment, but may pass as well. The facilitator summarizes and/or charts the round, capturing important themes and ideas that emerged from the discussion. ○ Round 3: *Reflective questions* The facilitator collects lingering questions from group members, and the host does not respond until the next round. ○ Round 4: *Response from the host* The lab host responds to the groups' questions and then shares thoughts for next steps for instruction. ○ Round 5: *Next steps* In a whip-around, each group member states a next step for his or her own work that arose from the observation. The facilitator takes notes for future follow-up and coaching.

Figure 6.4   Protocol for Peer Learning Labs

Prebriefing Session (30 minutes)	• The lab host shares the focus question and provides background and context to the observers. The facilitator discusses norms for the observation and participants ask clarifying questions.
Observation (50–60 minutes)	• Observers take notes that are specific to the host's focus question.

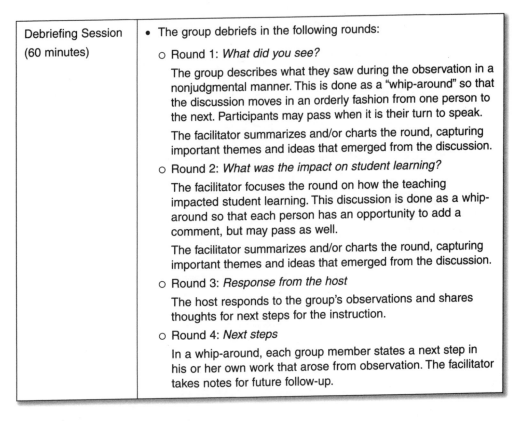

Debriefing Session (60 minutes)	• The group debriefs in the following rounds:
	○ Round 1: *What did you see?*
	The group describes what they saw during the observation in a nonjudgmental manner. This is done as a "whip-around" so that the discussion moves in an orderly fashion from one person to the next. Participants may pass when it is their turn to speak.
	The facilitator summarizes and/or charts the round, capturing important themes and ideas that emerged from the discussion.
	○ Round 2: *What was the impact on student learning?*
	The facilitator focuses the round on how the teaching impacted student learning. This discussion is done as a whip-around so that each person has an opportunity to add a comment, but may pass as well.
	The facilitator summarizes and/or charts the round, capturing important themes and ideas that emerged from the discussion.
	○ Round 3: *Response from the host*
	The host responds to the group's observations and shares thoughts for next steps for the instruction.
	○ Round 4: *Next steps*
	In a whip-around, each group member states a next step in his or her own work that arose from observation. The facilitator takes notes for future follow-up.

Designing Learning Labs

Learning labs are best designed collaboratively by a principal, coach, and possibly some teacher leaders using the following checklist:

Figure 6.5   A Checklist for Designing Learning Labs

Yes/No	Have we determined our purpose for implementing learning labs?
Yes/No	Have we identified lab hosts based on the criteria for the particular type of lab we are implementing?
Yes/No	Has the lab host been provided with support from the coach, such as spending time in the classroom and planning the focus question and look for's?
Yes/No	In the weeks leading up to the observation, has the coach provided extra coaching support to the lab host such as through a six- to nine-week coaching cycle?
Yes/No	Has release time been scheduled for the observing teachers and lab host (usually a half day to allow for the prebrief, observation, and debrief)?
Yes/No	Have observers been prepared with a protocol and norms for the observation?
Yes/No	After the observation, did the coach follow up with the lab host and participants on next steps that came out of the process?

Observation Norms and Note-Taking Tool

More often than not, inappropriate behavior is the result of a lack of information among the lab participants. Therefore, it is up to the facilitator to frame what is expected among the observers using the following materials.

Figure 6.6   Observation Norms

- Record detailed notes that are aligned with the observation and will inform the debriefing session.
- Stay close to the action so you can see and hear what students are doing as learners.
- Only talk with students if it has been established as a part of the process for collecting evidence by the lab host and facilitator.
- Avoid being a distraction in the classroom. Maintain silence and do not take it upon yourself to teach the students.
- Maintain a positive attitude and respect for the lab host.

Figure 6.7   Note-Taking Tool for Student-Centered Labs

Teacher:	
Facilitator:	
School:	
Date:	
Focus	
Look For's	

	Student Evidence	Instructional Practices
Next Steps for Instruction & Assessment		
Lingering Questions & Support Needed		

Figure 6.8 Tips for Facilitating Observations

- Use a protocol for all classroom observations.
- If a group member fails to follow the protocol, revisit the steps in the protocol, specifically pointing out the purpose for each step in the process.
- In advance of the observation, spend time in the classroom where the observation will take place.
- Work with the host teacher to craft a focus question and look for's that will propel the thinking of the group.
- Hone your skills at probing and paraphrasing—these are the two most useful skills for lab facilitators.
- Don't hesitate to refer back to the norms for observation.

A Final Thought

Bringing a group of classroom teachers, principals, and coaches to observe in Nicole's special education classroom led to insights that nobody would have expected. Though they are struggling learners, Nicole's students exceeded our expectations for what kids can do. Nicole didn't say "yes" to hosting visitors because she wanted to be viewed as an expert. Instead, she agreed because she wanted more insight into how writing about their problem solving would support them as mathematicians. And as a result of the experience, Nicole gained new thinking about her students and every other person, no matter what his or her role, did too. Learning labs are yet another example of the power that comes from student-centered collaboration among teachers, principals, and coaches.

7

Developing Systems and Structures for Teacher Learning

When I was a child, my mother used an old aluminum pressure cooker—she was a working mom and was looking for ways to speed up our dinner preparations. Once, it built up too much pressure and exploded right there in the kitchen, splattering beef stew over every square inch of the walls and ceiling. I don't think my mother ever used it again and thanks to modern conveniences like microwaves and crockpots, pressure cookers have gone the way of the record player and typewriter.

As a result of initiatives including No Child Left Behind, our schools have taken on some of the same characteristics of my mother's pressure cooker. They are implementing a myriad of programs, assessments, and interventions at a record pace. The learning curve is steep and for the first time in my educational career, I have come across well-intentioned teachers breaking down in tears because they can't do it all.

Some pressure can be a good thing when it comes to improving schools. Michael Fullan has written about the importance of finding a balance between pressure and support—a theory that was implemented on a large scale by Tony Blair, then Prime Minister of England, to reform England's schools. Fullan writes (2009),

> What was more significant was that Blair and his team, led by chief architect of strategy, Michael Barber, said that they would base their strategy on existing *change knowledge*, by that they meant they would combine "pressure and support"—the *pressure* of targets, monitoring progress, feeding back data, and intervening in cases of low performance; *support* meant investing in "capacity building" through establishing new positions at the school, district, and government levels to lead literacy and numeracy through intensive professional learning opportunities focusing on instructional improvement and through the development and spread of new high quality curriculum materials. (p. 3)

Finding the right balance isn't easy. Some pressure can speed up the process (like our beef stew) . . . but too much can create a big mess. In this chapter you'll be introduced to ideas for developing a student-centered system for professional development that moves a school forward while also managing the needs of the individuals within it.

A Student-Centered Framework for Professional Development

How do school leaders provide teachers with the support they need and also increase student achievement? In a student-centered model of professional development, the primary focus is on a specific goal or target for student learning. This is a departure from the past in which professional development typically focused on the implementation of a set of teaching practices and then made the assumption that these practices would trickle down to increased student learning.

It's time to rethink the goals we have for professional development. Anthony Muhammad (2009) writes,

> The reauthorization in 2001 of the Elementary and Secondary Education Act (ESEA), also known as No Child Left Behind (NCLB), symbolized a huge shift in the focus of America's schools. This bill, which requires that all students

in America's public schools perform at a proficient level on each state's standardized assessment in reading and mathematics by 2014 or face sanctions, sent a shockwave through the U.S. public school system. The introduction of this legislation meant that for the first time in U.S. history, schools would be judged based upon *student outcomes*, not *educator intentions*. (p. 9)

Professional development is the last frontier in our shift to emphasizing student outcomes over educator intentions. By thinking *first* about a goal for students and then designing the support for teachers, we can redefine professional development to ensure that it meets the needs of our students and teachers (Figure 7.1).

Figure 7.1 A Student-Centered Framework for Professional Development

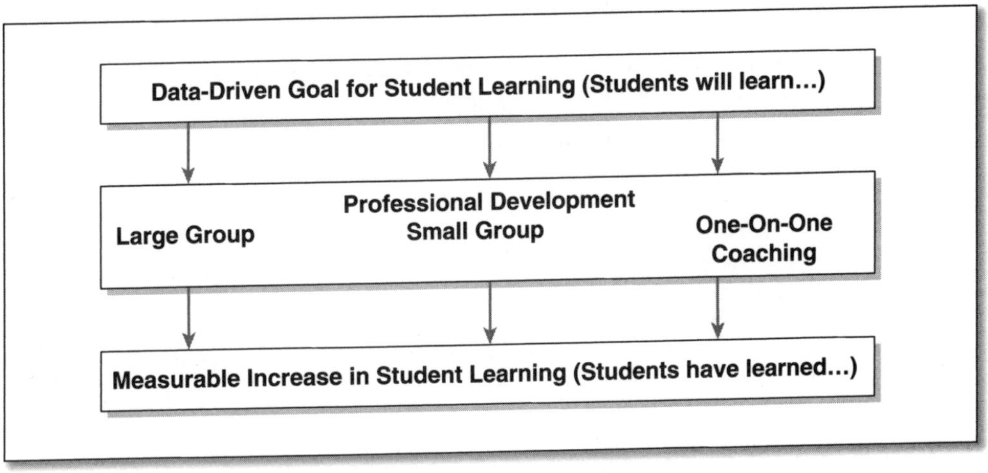

The Three Venues for Professional Development

The Three Venues for Professional Development differentiates support through a variety of professional development formats (large group, small group, and one-on-one coaching) that meet the diverse needs of teachers. When used in conjunction with a goal for student learning, the Three Venues for Professional Development provides the principal, coach, and teachers with a predictable and results-based framework of support (Figure 7.2).

Figure 7.2   Three Venues for Professional Development

Large-Group Sessions include the full faculty or combined departments or teams. In the early stages, these sessions involve the use of data to set clear and measurable goals for students. When a goal is in place, the faculty shifts to research and develop teaching practices that will accomplish the goal. Practices for this venue include

- data analysis to identify a goal for student learning;
- investigation of resources such as teaching practices, programs, or curriculum that will directly target the students' needs; and
- the use of professional development strategies such as classroom observations, professional reading, or other forms of discussion to develop the teachers' abilities to address the students' needs in the classroom.

Small-Group Sessions include smaller teams, such as by grade level or department. At this stage, teams move through a continuous loop of reflection on student data and teaching practices to assess the impact and make adjustments. Practices for this venue include

- the use of data teams and assessment walls to continually analyze student progress;
- coaching cycles with teams of teachers;
- protocol-based discussions to develop and share teaching practices that align with the goal for student learning; and
- peer-based observations, further orientation to resources, and study groups to refine the teaching practice.

One-On-One Coaching includes individuals or pairs of teachers. This venue is individualized and focuses on the needs of specific students and teachers. Practices for this venue include

- collaborative and continual analysis of student evidence or data;
- coaching that may include demonstration teaching, co-teaching, or observation by the coach; and
- ongoing planning conversations by the coach and teacher.

A Case Study in Student-Centered Professional Development: Goldrick Elementary

When the principal and coaches from Goldrick Elementary sat down with the data that had just arrived from the Colorado Department of Education, it would have been easy for them to become overwhelmed. In spite of their efforts, it was clear that many of their students were not performing adequately on the state reading test and something had to be done.

Located in southwest Denver, and with a student population in which 88% of the students speak a language other than English and 85% qualify for free or reduced lunch, Goldrick was under pressure to help all students reach proficiency in reading, writing, and mathematics. It is a school with a fairly young and energetic staff of teachers, three coaches, and a committed school leader.

Laurie, the principal at Goldrick, began by pulling the coaches together to create a plan for professional development. A plan that took shape as they thought through the following questions (Figure 7.3).

Figure 7.3 Guiding Questions for Planning Student-Centered Professional Development

- How will we process through the data to determine a professional development focus? What data will inform this decision?
- How will we build ownership among the teachers as they engage in the process?
- What student work or assessment data will we use to measure progress?
- How will we provide support to teachers?
- How long do we think it will take to reach our goal?
- How will we measure the impact of the professional development on students?
- How will the principal, coach, and leadership team collaborate?

The team decided to begin by leading the full staff through a close examination of the state assessment data. They learned that a majority of students were struggling to summarize the text they were encountering on the test—a discovery that established an overarching focus for professional development that stretched over a few months.

With the focus in place, Laurie and the coaches worked together to develop a differentiated plan for professional development that included a variety of professional development activities. They grouped teachers in a flexible manner and were careful to maintain the focus on summarization as a common thread for shared learning (Figure 7.4).

Figure 7.4 Three Venues Planning Tool for Goldrick Elementary

Professional Development Activities		
Whole Group	**Small Group**	**One-On-One**
• analysis of assessment data • goal setting for students • introduction to resources	• examining student work • weekly grade-level meetings • professional reading groups • vertical/cross-grade-level teams • further exploration of resources • new teacher team meetings	• coaching cycles • demonstration, co-teaching, and observation • co-planning • examining student work aligned with standards • application of resources

Data analysis was a core practice and was guided by age-appropriate and informal assessments that were developed by the coaches. Mostly written responses to reading, the assessments were used throughout the school on a monthly basis and were analyzed in grade-level teams. Then, with the help of the coaching team, the teaching was adjusted to address any student needs that came to light.

As the teachers administered the informal assessments, they were able to identify growth in the skills required for summarization. This motivated the teachers, as they could easily connect how the work they were doing was directly affecting their students. The conversations about the assessments also raised some important issues for the teachers and coaches, such as questions about the level of text the students are reading in the classroom as compared with what they would encounter on the state test, concerns about vocabulary development with their population of mostly second-language learners, and some discussion about how their ongoing work with reading comprehension dovetailed with what was required for summarization.

Individualized support was also provided through ongoing coaching cycles and informal planning sessions. And a specialized study group for the first-year teachers was established so the newest members of the staff could get the specialized support they needed.

What seemed to be a simple skill—summarization—proved to be complex and important work for the teachers to tackle as a learning community. As the school leader, Laurie worked with the coaches to use data and craft a focus for professional development that was based on the needs of the students. And when the students took the state reading test in the spring, the teachers' hard work paid off with the third-grade students making gains of over 20 percentage points on the reading test followed by a 17% increase by the fourth graders a year later—not bad.

Coaching as an Essential Element of Professional Development

School-based coaches play a critical role in helping teachers reach their goals for students. They build capacity by providing direct, continual, and student-centered support, and without this support, efforts at school reform have little chance of raising student achievement. That said, coaching that is poorly designed, that doesn't clearly define the coaches' role, and that isn't directly connected with the larger goals of the organization will also have little effect.

School leaders who understand the differing and multifaceted roles of a coach can leverage those roles for greater impact. For example, the coach can actively lead dialogue and reflection using student data. Killion and Harrison identify this role as a "data coach" and write (2006), "In this role, coaches help teams of teachers and/or individual teachers to examine data, understand their students' strengths and weaknesses, and identify instructional strategies, structures, programs, or curriculum to address identified needs" (p. 35).

By defining data coach as a distinct role, the school leader is in a position to match this role with relevant professional development structures, such as coaching with student work, facilitating conversations at the assessment wall, or creating assessments to monitor progress. Now the school community understands the role of the coach and how it relates to specific structures for professional development. Other roles for coaches that lend themselves to specific professional development structures include the following:

- The coach as facilitator. This role rests on the assumption that the school has allocated collaborative time for teams and/or groups of teachers. When this is the case, a skilled facilitator will increase the outcomes of group work. Professional development structures that match this role are dialogue and reflection among teams of teachers, learning labs or classroom observations, and other forms of professional learning among groups of teachers.
- The coach as co-teacher. Co-teaching puts the coach right alongside the teacher as instruction is delivered. When coaches are defined as co-teachers, their role to provide individualized support to teachers is reinforced. It also provides the coach with credibility and helps teachers see the coach as a person who will roll up his or her sleeves and do the hard work of teaching.

A systems framework for professional development calls for the careful integration of a series of moving parts that interact and influence one another. By carefully designing the diverse roles of a coach alongside a framework for professional development, we create a synchronized system in which all the parts work together.

The Important Role of Teacher Leaders

Investing in teacher leaders builds school capacity and creates conditions for change that will endure. Teacher leaders provide invaluable insight into how school reforms, a new curriculum or program, and other initiatives are being translated to the classroom on a daily basis with students. We can benefit from believing in teacher leaders, trusting their judgment, and asking their opinion . . . something that we sometimes forget to do when we are in the midst of an improvement effort.

The role of the teacher leader is distinct from that of the principal. According to Charlotte Danielson (2005),

> There is nothing in the concept of teacher leadership that conflicts with the important (indeed essential) role of administrative leadership. Site administrators are, after all, the people in charge of the building; they are the managers and see to it that operations run smoothly. But they also do much more: They set the tone, they maintain the focus on student learning, they create a culture of professional inquiry and an expectation that all teachers will be involved in ongoing improvement of the school's program. They are, along with being managers, the instructional leaders of their schools. (p. 36)

Coaches play a critical role in fostering teacher leaders. For example, a coach may encourage teachers to get involved in leadership teams, solicit the voices and opinions of a broad cast of teachers, and consider the viewpoints of these teachers when designing and implementing professional development. Coaches also benefit from participating themselves in leadership teams as it provides the opportunity to serve as a decision-maker within the school community.

Teacher leaders can be grown at the school level, or they can be cultivated off-site through university partnerships or district-level initiatives. The transition to teacher leader can be awkward as teachers move from a child-centered viewpoint to one in which they are fully engaged with their peers. This may require a new set of skills for teachers who choose to transition into a leadership role. In *Learning Along the Way* (2003), I write,

> Although teachers are quite comfortable working with children, leadership requires an entirely different set of skills. When the best teachers are plucked from the classroom to become instructional leaders among their peers, they rarely receive any guidance about how to work with other adults. Teacher leaders need to be trained in strategies for working with adult learners. They need a repertoire of facilitation

frameworks, protocols for leading adults in discussion, and even the most basic information about how to organize their time in a new role. (p. 88)

The following curriculum outlines steps a school, district, or outside agency can use to encourage the development of teacher leaders (Figure 7.5).

Figure 7.5 A Curriculum for Developing Teacher Leaders

Roles for Teacher Leaders	Suggested Support for Teacher Leaders
Facilitating Small-Group Collaboration	• Practice and experience using a variety of collaborative processes, protocols, and norm-setting procedures • Strategies for maintaining focus during group work • Intervention techniques for facilitating difficult conversations • Tools and strategies for planning group work • Strategies for evaluating the impact of group work
Piloting New Programs or Initiatives	• Early exposure to new materials • Problem solving related to the implementation of new materials • Observations of new materials as they are in use • Coaching cycles based on the use of new materials • Group work with others who are piloting new materials, such as problem solving and sharing of ideas • Group work to suggest adaptations to a new program based on the teacher leaders' experience
Sharing Craft Knowledge and Expertise	• Varied opportunities to participate in a school culture in which *all* teachers are encouraged to share craft knowledge • Participation in learning labs (model classrooms or peer learning labs) as the lab host or observer • Coaching cycles or informal coaching conversations
Hosting Learning Labs (model classrooms or peer learning labs)	• Support from the coach to plan for an upcoming observation • Coaching cycles in advance of an observation to deepen reflection and implementation • Resources to support teacher leaders to articulate the research that drives their instruction • Exposure and practice with the protocol that will be used for an observation • (For more on learning labs, see Chapter 6)

(Continued)

Figure 7.5 (Continued)

Roles for Teacher Leaders	Suggested Support for Teacher Leaders
Facilitating Learning Labs (model classrooms or peer learning labs)	• Strategies for maintaining focus during observations • Intervention techniques for difficult groups • Strategies for working with the host teacher to design an observation • Strategies for evaluating the impact of an observation • Exposure and practice with the protocol that will be used for an observation
Serving on Leadership and/or Data Teams	• The development of a "big picture" perspective rather than a singular view of one's own classroom and needs • Clearly defined expectations for the teacher leader's role on the team • A clearly defined framework or process for team work • Strategies for voicing one's opinion in a productive manner
Mentoring New Teachers	• A mentoring program that aligns with the requirements for teacher induction • The development of a specific set of skills for mentoring new teachers • Instruction in working with adult learners (male/female, and across generations and processing styles) • Strategies for record keeping, documentation, and communication with mentees • (For more on working with adult learners, see Chapter 8)
Leading Professional Development Sessions	• Tools, technologies, and techniques for presentation • Instruction in working with adult learners (male/female, and across generations and processing styles) • Practice with a variety of collaborative processes, protocols, and norm-setting procedures • Strategies for maintaining focus for large groups • Intervention techniques for difficult groups • Tools and strategies for planning professional development • Strategies for evaluating the impact of professional development
Becoming a Nationally Board-Certified Teacher	• Support and incentives from the district level to become nationally board certified • Opportunities for collaboration within the school or across the district with others who are engaged in the process • Learning labs (model classrooms or peer learning labs) within the cadre of teachers who are engaged in the process
Fostering the School Learning Community	• Encourage teacher leaders to view and present themselves as learners rather than experts • Promote a climate of questioning and inquiry • Define teacher leaders as those who reflect and ask questions rather than as those who have all the answers

What About the "Tougher" Teachers?

Developing systems for professional development means we have to think carefully about the full scope of teachers that we find in our schools. Inevitably, there are those who are on board and willing to engage as learners. And there are others who aren't. In his research on school culture, Anthony Muhammad (2009) observed in 34 schools across the country to determine how the schools functioned as learning communities and how these behaviors influenced student achievement. Through his research, he identified four distinct groups that we find in most school communities and determined that these groups have an enormous influence on change efforts within schools:

- The Believers. Believers hold high expectations for their students and believe that these expectations can be achieved. For the most part, they have been practicing teachers for more than three years and, as Muhammad writes, "They have made a decision to accept a student-centered paradigm as their primary mode of operation, regardless of outside opposition" (p. 31).
- The Tweeners. Tweeners are newer to the school culture and may be influenced by either the Believers or the negative teachers on staff. For the most part, Tweeners are eager to please, compliant, and want to do what's best for their students, though they may not be quite sure what that is.
- The Survivors. Survivors are a specific, and small, population of teachers who are unhappy as educators. They are unlikely to fully engage in efforts toward school improvement because they don't have the energy or interest to take on these types of challenges.
- The Fundamentalists. Fundamentalists are firmly rooted in a single definition of "schooling" and expect any necessary adjustments to be made by the students, rather than by them. As Muhammad describes them, these "are staff members who are not only opposed to change, but organize to resist and thwart any change initiative. They can wield tremendous political power and are a major obstacle in implementing meaningful school reform. They actively work against the Believers" (p. 29).

I once observed a coaching session with a middle school language arts teacher who had asked her coach to help her shift away from whole-class novels to allow more choice and help the students practice their reading strategies across different types of texts. On the surface, this was a pretty typical coaching conversation: they talked about their goals for the students as readers and brainstormed some lesson ideas. Under the surface was a far more complex issue. Jenny was a new teacher and was on a team of Fundamentalists. They didn't like it one bit that she had departed from the list of class novels that they had been using for the past decade, and had embarked on a campaign of intimidation to make sure she towed the line.

On the surface, Jamie's role as coach was to help Jenny design a few lessons. But in truth, it turned out to be a covert operation in which they were flying under the radar to plan instruction that would best meet the needs of Jenny's students. In spite of the Fundamentalists on her team, I could see that Jenny was on her way to becoming a Believer . . . if she made it that far.

If we want to truly effect change, every member of a school community must join in the effort to elevate our expectations for students and ward off the negativism and hostility that some teachers bring to our school communities. Principals can set the tone that the students' needs come before the teachers' personal beliefs. Coaches can help to build capacity throughout the school. And teacher leaders can ban together in an effort to shift the school culture toward one that believes in kids.

Teacher Evaluation

Teacher evaluation is a formal process that is directly linked to job retention, promotion, and tenure. The well-intentioned purpose of teacher evaluation is to hold teachers accountable for implementing specific practices in their classrooms. Yet the reality is it often feels like a time-intensive process that does very little to promote student learning.

You've read many examples of how professional development can be shifted to a student-centered approach in which goals for students drive the instructional decision making. The same can be said for teacher evaluation (Figures 7.6 and 7.7).

Most school-based coaches do not administer teacher evaluations. However, their work is often impacted by the evaluation process since they are the primary source of support for teachers. By shifting to a student-centered approach, teachers are guided toward making decisions based on targets for student learning rather than on a specific program or philosophy of teaching. These conversations set the wheels in motion for a coach to step in and provide ongoing support through student-centered coaching.

Figure 7.6   Traditional Teacher Evaluation Compared With Student-Centered Teacher Evaluation

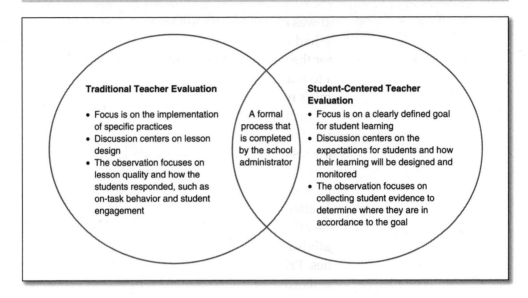

Figure 7.7   Student-Centered Teacher Evaluation Form

Teacher Name	Observer Name
Grade/Subject	School
Pre Conference Date	Time
Observation Date	Time
Post Conference Date	Time

Pre Conference

1. What are your goals for the students during the time in which you will be observed?

2. What have you done in the past that relates to this goal?

3. How does the goal connect to the standards and curriculum for your grade/subject?

4. What do you expect to see students doing in relationship to the goal?

Figure 7.7 (Continued)

5. Will you provide any individuals or groups of students with extra assistance (ELL, special education, etc.)? If so, how?

6. Do you have any students who may need other forms of instruction (i.e., gifted, etc.)?

7. How would you like me to collect student evidence during the observation?

Observation

Observations of Student Learning

Observations of Teacher Practice

Post Conference

1. What was observed that provides evidence of student learning that relates to the teacher's goal?

2. What was observed that indicated the need for follow-up by the teacher?

3. In what ways did the teaching practice move student learning forward?

4. What was observed that indicated the need for further development of teacher practice?

5. What resources is the school prepared to provide to support the development of teacher practice?

Meanwhile . . . in the Principal's Office

It seems counterintuitive, but in schools with a coach, it is vitally important for principals to spend time in classrooms. Principals who develop their own context for what is occurring in classrooms are able to identify needs among teachers and work collaboratively with the coach to address those needs. Without their own knowledge of what's taking place in classrooms, principals may inadvertently rely on the coach for this information and will likely damage the coach's relationships with teachers.

Being in classrooms requires principals to understand and recognize what they should be looking for in terms of teaching and learning. This has become increasingly challenging as we adopt more sophisticated models of instruction—changes that have made it necessary for principals to develop their own pedagogical knowledge across multiple subject areas. Principals who aren't able to keep up may have a hard time gaining meaning from classroom visits.

Formats for Classroom Visits

Walkthroughs are a common format for classroom visits. City, Elmore, Fiarman, and Teitel share the concerns many educators have about walkthroughs and write,

> Unfortunately, the practice of walkthroughs has become corrupted in many ways by confounding it with the supervision and evaluation of teachers. The purpose of some walkthroughs has been to identify deficiencies in classroom practice and to "fix" teachers who manifest these deficiencies. In many instances, judgments about what needs fixing are made on the basis of simplistic checklists that have little or nothing to do with the direct experience of teachers in their classrooms. Groups of administrators descend on classrooms with clipboards and checklists, caucus briefly in the hallway, and then deliver a set of simplistic messages about what needs fixing. (2009, p. 4)

I once worked in a large, urban district that implemented this type of walkthrough. In my work to support a team of twelve literacy coaches, I saw firsthand the type of fallout that was created when these walkthroughs took place—teachers were frantic, worried, and distrustful; the coaches weren't sure of their role in the process; and unfortunately very little positive growth occurred.

After this experience, I have become gun-shy of walkthroughs, yet I still believe in the importance of a school leader who knows intimately what learning is looking like in each and every classroom in a school. The following practices for classroom visits can take us beyond those days of clipboard-carrying teams of administrators and hold promise for moving increasing student achievement while honoring a culture of learning.

Instructional Rounds

In their book *Instructional Rounds in Education* (2009), City, Elmore, Fiarman, and Teitel introduce instructional rounds as a counterpoint to walkthroughs. The instructional rounds process is based on medical rounds in which "groups of medical interns, residents, and supervising or attending physicians visit patients, observe and discuss the evidence of diagnoses, and, after a thorough analysis of the evidence, discuss possible treatments," (p. 3) and include the following elements:

- Work is performed by teams (or networks) of educators and is driven by a "problem of practice" that is identified by the network.
- The problem of practice is observable and connects to the school's plan for teaching and learning.
- The observation relates directly to the problem of practice and is nonevaluative and descriptive.
- The observation is debriefed in the following actions: description of what was seen, analysis of the descriptive evidence, and predictions of what the impact will be on student learning.
- Coupled with the observation is a process of shared learning in which the team determines next steps for the school or district.

A departure from teacher-centered types of walkthroughs, instructional rounds take a student-centered approach to build capacity around specific goals for student learning and then develop a plan to address the students' needs. This is done through a collaborative and nonjudgmental approach that contributes to a school culture that is based on student achievement.

The Three-Minute Walkthrough

In the book *The Three-Minute Classroom Walk-Through: Changing School Supervisory Practice One Teacher at a Time* (2004), Downey, Steffy, English, Frase, and Poston developed a format for walkthroughs that includes the following characteristics:

- Observations are brief, informal, and last three to four minutes and are performed by the school administrator.
- The focus of the three-minute walkthrough is on teacher decision making, reflection, and professional growth rather than for purposes of teacher evaluation.
- Feedback is provided in a written form or through dialogue and occurs after eight to ten observations rather than after one classroom visit.
- The walkthrough is not driven by a checklist or rubric.

The intention of the three-minute walkthrough is for principals to visit classrooms regularly and informally in order to reflect with teachers, develop their own pedagogical expertise, and establish a school culture that is open and reflective. Three minutes may not seem like very much time, but if a series of short classroom visits are strung together, then a holistic picture will emerge.

Tools and Techniques

Agenda Design Tool for Teacher Leaders

Teacher leaders are often familiar with planning instruction for their students and are far less comfortable doing so for the adult learners in their school. The following tool supports teacher leaders to design and implement student-centered professional development.

Figure 7.8   Agenda Design Tool

1. Establish purposes and outcomes for the session. What are our goals for the students?

2. Establish expectations. Which of the following matches the role(s) for each member of the group?

   ___ receiving information to build our awareness
   ___ serving as an advisory body to inform the process on a broader scale
   ___ serving as a decision-making body
   ___ leading the process for others
   ___ other_____

3. Develop content. What will be the new or ongoing learning for the group? How will this impact our students?

4. Develop techniques and instructional processes. How will the group interact with the material?

A Final Thought

As educators, we know that a primary requirement for success in the 21st century is a sound education. The goal of No Child Left Behind, to achieve proficiency among all students, is lofty and intimidating— but essential. And the pressure we are under as educators has no doubt created improved opportunities for many of our students.

In our 1970s kitchen, my mother's pressure cooker did speed things along. And our schools can also benefit from pressure when it is coupled with specific, intentional, and focused professional development and support. This is far from easy, but by working together, principals, coaches, and teachers can carefully design and implement professional development that balances these two essential components (pressure and support) without leaving a mess to clean up.

8

Engaging the Adult Learner

Fraser, Colorado, lies at 8,500 feet above sea level at the base of the Continental Divide. Mountains encircle this high alpine valley of rocky outcroppings, aspen trees, and a peculiar type of mountain folk who relish the fact that they live in a town with the official nickname, "The Icebox of the Nation." Flatlanders are often intimidated by the ruggedness of the area. Moose and bear sightings are common and hikers routinely get lost on the vast network of trails. I'm one of those peculiar people who love this place. And when I'm not working, I am here on my skis, snowshoes, or mountain bike.

It's a crisp and clear morning in late September. Cyndy and I are panting our way up a trail on our mountain bikes. An avid adventure seeker, Cyndy often coaxes me to take on new challenges. When I hear her say, "Let's not ride the same old thing, let's try something new!" I am filled with dread. Riding something new could mean we end up getting hopelessly lost on the more than 600 miles of trails in the area. Or we could tackle something that is too hard—and maybe I don't feel like working that hard. I begrudgingly agree, mostly because I don't want to let her down, but just to be safe, I tuck a trail map into in my backpack before leaving the house.

When Cyndy's not around, I stick to a few trails where I am comfortable. But she encourages me to take risks. We need people in our life like Cyndy: people who push us out of our comfort zone and toward new learning. Our inner voice may be screaming, "This is too hard," or "I might fail!" but somehow we find the courage to take that step.

Every day we ask teachers to take on new learning that they may be less than comfortable with. We give accolades to teachers who are go-getters like Cyndy. These are the adventure seekers whose little voices of fear and doubt don't slow them down a bit. Likewise, we are frustrated by colleagues who approach new learning with trepidation. We wonder why they aren't trying new things or are reluctant about new programs and initiatives. Why are we so impatient with the fear and reticence that is intrinsic to new learning when we ought to come to expect it? This chapter examines this question by taking a closer look at how to motivate and encourage the adult learner toward fearless learning.

Risk, Relationship, and Coaching

Risk is unavoidable if we are to embark on a learning path. Learners have to, as Roland Barth (2007) puts it, "risk disclosing to the world that they don't know how and that they intend to learn how." He writes,

> I have suggested conditions necessary for getting learning curves off the chart—observation of practice, conversation about practice, reflection and writing about practice, telling stories, sharing craft knowledge, and maximizing the difference in order to maximize learning. Each of them invites, even demands, profound levels of risk taking. The ultimate risk is to disclose ourselves. (p. 214)

When asking others to stare down the risk, fear, and discomfort that is associated with new learning, we can create an island of safety within the sea of change. Remembering that every adult learner is different (much like the children in our classrooms), we can create scaffolds that ease them into learning gracefully. We have discussed that the primary ingredient to helping others take on risk is a trusting and respectful relationship. But then what?

Early on in my first job as a literacy coach, I assumed that teachers would line up eagerly for my help. What I found is some did, but not everyone. Instead, I ended up with a mix of eager teachers (who probably would have signed up for anything), somewhat skeptical teachers (who participated on their own terms), and teachers who dodged me whenever they saw me walking down the hall. I didn't have any idea of what to do, so I focused on the ones who were on board and avoided the rest. The Flow of Coaching (Flaherty, 1999) helped me answer this question and better understand the stages teachers go through as they prepare to engage in coaching. With this knowledge, I could better manage the process and work systematically to scaffold teachers into risk taking in a way that honored them as individuals and as learners (Figure 8.1).

Figure 8.1   Flow of Coaching

Establish Relationships

The coach builds a trusting, respectful, and collegial relationship to serve as the foundation for the coaching work. Relationships are developed through the following types of activities:

- Learn alongside teachers in large and small groups
- Collect, manage, and share materials with teachers
- Support teachers with assessments
- Develop strategies for creating and sustaining the classroom community
- Get to know students and teachers by spending time in their classrooms

Recognize Openings

As the relationship develops, the coach listens carefully for openings from teachers. Openings come in the form of direct requests for coaching, challenges that teachers are having, or a more subtle request for help. The key is recognizing that openings for coaching come from the teacher and not from the coach. However, they can be triggered in the following ways:

- Participate in small- and large-group sessions and listen for teachers to name their needs in the context of other learning
- Survey teachers regarding their needs
- Share coaching opportunities with teachers
- Check in informally to see how things are going for teachers

Familiarize Yourself With the Classroom Context

As soon as a coach has an opening from a teacher, the coach learns more about the classroom environment by spending time during the relevant instructional period. This provides the coach with the ability to do the following:

- Develop relationships with the students to build trust with the teacher
- Identify strengths that can be built on with the teacher
- Familiarize herself or himself with the teacher's practices so he or she can integrate into the classroom in a seamless fashion

Create Agreements With the Teacher

At this stage, the coach and teacher engage in a process of developing a set of agreements for their work together. This discussion centers on topics such as the following:

- A shared focus for the work
- The teacher's hopes and possible fears related to coaching
- A discussion about what the coach needs from the teacher, and vice versa
- Agreements about scheduling

Engage in Coaching Conversations

With a trusting relationship, an opening from the teacher, an understanding of the classroom context, and agreements in place, the coach and teacher are ready to engage in coaching work that can include the following:

- Ongoing coaching cycles with individuals
- Informal coaching

Adapted from James Flaherty, *Coaching: Evoking Excellence in Others.* (Butterworth-Heinemann, 1999).

Coaching Across Generations

Understanding the differences between generational groups is essential to coaching across the school community. Today's workplace includes members of four separate and distinct generations. *Traditionalists,* born between 1900 and 1945, include about 75 million people. *Baby Boomers* make up the largest group of about 80 million people who were born between 1946 and 1964. *Generation X* is a much smaller group of approximately 46 million who were born between 1965 and 1980. The *Millennials (or Generation Y)* are almost as large as the Baby Boomers, with at least 76 million people who were born between 1981 and 1999.

In the book *When Generations Collide,* Lancaster and Stillman (2002) write,

> For years people have analyzed factors like age, life stage, gender, race, ethnicity, socioeconomic status, religion, educational background, thinking styles, Myers-Briggs profiles, and even signs of the zodiac to find ways to understand each other better. Yet somehow we've failed to recognize the form of diversity that affects every human being on a daily basis— *generational differences.* (p. 13)

Differences that are based on common experiences and a common history that is shared by each generational group.

Traditionalists were shaped by World War I and II, the New Deal, the Great Depression, and the GI Bill, which provided a college education to millions. They experienced society rallying around common causes and coming out victorious, which created a hardworking and patriotic generation that views our institutions with loyalty and reverence. This is illustrated by the heroes to the Traditionalists: Franklin Delano Roosevelt, John Wayne, and Joe DiMaggio.

Baby Boomers benefited from the opportunity that came with the booming postwar economy of the 1940s to 1960s as well as from their idealistic and well-educated parents. Due to this generation's vast size, it didn't take long for Baby Boomers to learn that they had to put in the necessary hours at work to stay competitive, making them a generation of hardworking achievers. They also applied their competitive prowess to raising their children and were the first generation to be termed "helicopter parents." Events that influenced Baby Boomers include the war in Vietnam, the civil rights movement, and the assassinations of Martin Luther King and John F. Kennedy.

As mostly the children of Baby Boomers, Generation X watched their parents work hard, sometimes at the cost of personal relationships. The divorce rate tripled during the birth years of Generation X. They have witnessed numerous corporate takeovers, mergers, and down-sizings and are painfully aware of the fact that Social Security, which they've been paying into with each paycheck, will be insolvent when they retire. These experiences, coupled with the empowerment they received from their doting parents, has led Generation X to grow up wondering if there isn't more to life. They are an independent and skeptical generation that depends on itself rather than on the very institutions that Traditionalists hold dear. Generation X is also the first generation to make striking a healthy balance between work and family a priority. And, thanks to advances in technology, they have figured out how to leverage conveniences like flexible scheduling and telecommuting so they can attend their children's parent teacher conferences or spring recitals . . . something that Baby Boomers would have never thought possible.

Just entering our teaching ranks are the Millennials, a group that has benefited from a healthy dose of attention and positive reinforcement from their Baby Boomer and Generation X parents. They are optimistic and idealistic and, until the recession of 2008, have grown up in a thriving economy. While Generation X has adapted to technology, the Millennials have never known life without it. A common joke among those of us who are trying to adjust to new technology is, "If you can't figure it out, just ask an eleven-year-old." We can't underestimate the impact technology has made on this generation. Where other generations define a conversation as a face-to-face interaction, Millennials view conversation as taking place in chat rooms, on social networks, or via text message.

Coaching across generations is particularly challenging as many of us hold a shared (and often negative) view of the *other* generations that we work alongside. Such negative stereotypes are rearing their ugly heads more often as schools make the shift toward increased collaboration. Labels such as the "in the box" or predictable Traditionalist, the overachieving Baby Boomer, the slacker Generation Xer, or the overly pampered Millennial don't help us better understand how to collaborate across generations but serve to further isolate us.

Understanding each generation is the first step, and rather than viewing the following patterns as absolutes or stereotypes, we can consider them as a tool for gaining deeper insight and to create opportunities for generational groups to engage in fearless learning—together (Figure 8.2). Lancaster and Stillman write, "While many generational

Figure 8.2   Coaching Across Generations

	View Coaching as . . .	Engage in Collaboration When . . .	Are Less Responsive to . . .
Traditionalists • Born before 1945 • 75 million people	Unnecessary. Traditionalists come from the school of hard knocks and expect to learn it the hard way.	It respects their age and level of experience.	Coaching that focuses on what they "should" be doing without respecting their experience. An approach that is too casual or lacks respect for the establishment.
Baby Boomers • Born between 1946 and 1964 • 80 million people	A welcome source of support. Baby Boomers will do whatever it takes to stay competitive.	It provides them with an advantage in the workplace.	Coaching that makes the Baby Boomer feel attacked and vulnerable by focusing on weaknesses or flaws. An approach that is too casual or that challenges their authority.
Generation X • Born between 1965 and 1980 • 46 million people	Generation X is interested in developing skills to further their career options. They may have a hard time finding the time for coaching as they work to find a work/family balance.	It shows or tells them what to do in an efficient manner, and it provides them with immediate feedback.	Coaching that is too round-about and doesn't get to the point quickly enough. They want to get feedback and move on. Rules and policies that seem to lead to inefficiencies or lack flexibility.
Millennials • Born after 1980 • 76 million people	A helpful way to adapt to the steep learning curve of becoming a teacher.	It provides them with support as they enter the workforce.	Coaching that is too theoretical and lacks the nuts and bolts related to teaching. Negativity or low expectations based on their age or experience level.

Adapted from Lancaster and Stillman, *When Generations Collide* (Harper Business, 2002).

experts have laid out age ranges to define the members of the generations, we believe these are just guidelines. There really is no magic birth date that makes you a part of a particular generation. Generational personalities go much deeper" (p. 13).

Addressing the diverse needs of the generational groups is quite a challenge. Can a coach possibly tailor their work to each individual's generational needs? Probably not. What a coach can do is develop an awareness of the patterns of generational groups and be sensitive to their needs. In Tools and Techniques at the end of this chapter, you'll find a survey to better understand the generational viewpoints of individuals, and an exercise to create dialogue about generational patterns and stereotypes with groups of people.

Coaching Across Gender

A few years ago, I joined a team of coaches in Edmonds, Washington, to discuss how to evaluate the impact of a districtwide literacy initiative. The district was interested in measuring the student impact of the project while taking into account the teachers' level of participation in professional development that included one-on-one coaching, study groups, classroom observations, and voluntary workshops. It took us several months to gather the data and when we finally sat down to look at it, we were surprised by a startling fact: male teachers were far less likely to participate in professional development and coaching than female teachers. We wondered why.

At around the same time, I had been mulling over the question I so often hear from coaches, "How do I get teachers to *buy in?*" And as serendipity would have it, in that very same week my husband brought home a book titled the *X and Y of Buy* by Elizabeth Pace (2009). He had learned about it in an interoffice training at the Fortune 500 insurance company where he worked. Amazingly enough, a book from the business world asked the same question: How do we better connect with both genders when selling a product? I immediately made the connection to coaching because as coaches we really are selling a product, and we can't settle for only reaching half of the population, can we?

In *The X and Y of Buy* (2009), Elizabeth Pace writes,

Men and women are different. The plumbing is different; the wiring is different. Not better . . . not worse . . . just different.

> We perceive, think, communicate, and respond to the world
> differently. To say this in a post-feminist corporate arena has
> been political suicide. Yet scientists have confirmed that men
> and women use different parts of their brains and thus behave
> differently in a host of situations. (p. 4)

Pace is quick to add that there are some exceptions to the rule—which
I think is especially true in a field like education. She writes, "We can
all agree that all men are not the same, and neither are all women
identical and the polar opposites of men. There are women with what
scientists call "male-differentiated" brains and men with "female-
differentiated brains—yes there are women who enjoy parallel park-
ing their cars" (p. xiv).

   In study after study, male and female brains have been proven
to be physically different. Dr. Leonard Sax (2009) writes, "In 2008,
researchers at UCLA concluded that at least some regions of the
cerebral cortex are organized in a fundamentally different way in
men and women." These physical variations are attributed to creating behavioral differences among men and women. The male
brain is about singular focus—taking on one task at a time and con-
quering it. Pace compares a man's brain to a file cabinet. Each of the
files, family, work, maintaining the car, managing finances, mow-
ing the lawn, and watching football, are separate things that never
make contact with each other. The male brain focuses on one thing
at a time and eschews multitasking. My husband is a perfect
example of this . . . lately his job has been hectic, demanding that
he be of service to multiple clients with multiple needs at the same
time. The files in his brain are overlapping and interrupting each
other all through the day, making him feel overwhelmed. Yet the
women in his office, with the exact same job, seem to have no problem working in this way. That's because the female brain is about
connectivity—all aspects of a problem are tended to and accounted
for *at once*. Pace explains that this is because a woman's brain is
more like a large table. Women see a complete picture of interre-
lated parts and pieces, and the files naturally overlap, connecting
things like family (don't forget to schedule a pediatrician's
appointment) with work (I'll move that meeting around and it
should be no problem). Given the differences in our brains, we realized that we had to find coaching practices that would resonate
with men and women if we wanted to make a greater impact on *all*
students (Figure 8.3).

Figure 8.3   Coaching Across Gender

Characteristic	Men	Women	Strategies for Coaching Men	Strategies for Coaching Women
View support as . . .	A threat or unnecessary exercise. Men typically do not want help; offering help insinuates that a man is weak.	A welcome source of support to improve as a professional.	Instead of offering "help," use action words, explaining how you will work together to solve a problem.	Women typically take all the help they can get.
Buys in when . . .	He knows what he is there to do and what the goals are.	She knows what she is there to do and how it relates to both her as an individual and the people around her.	Use action words like "This will increase student achievement by . . ."	Address both what the work will accomplish and how it will impact the people around her.
Communicates by . . .	Using words sparingly and speaking directly and to the point. Beating around the bush is seen as a sign of weakness or inefficiency.	Weaving through conversations that include anecdotes, personal stories, and examples. Getting to the point too quickly is seen as abrasive or abrupt.	Avoid interrupting men; it is an insult and a threat. Listen carefully and address their *stated* needs. Avoid addressing their *perceived* needs.	The female brain is language dependent. The average 20-month-old girl has twice the vocabulary of the average 20-month-old boy. Women interrupt each other frequently in order to confirm that they are listening and understanding.
Make decisions by . . .	Dividing the situation into separate parts and pieces, analyzing each piece, and then making a decision.	Considering each aspect of a problem and then synthesizing what seems to be relevant to make a decision.	Address the main point and eliminate fluff or unnecessary information.	Allow a woman the time she needs to cull through the necessary information.

(Continued)

Figure 8.3 (Continued)

Characteristic	Men	Women	Strategies for Coaching Men	Strategies for Coaching Women
Prefers to sit . . .	Shoulder to shoulder	Face to face	Face to face communication can be uncomfortable and viewed as confrontational for some men.	Women prefer to sit face to face, to have full view of the other's facial expressions so that they can make a connection with others.
Responds to stress by . . .	Fight or flight	Tend and befriend	In stressful times, men prefer to be alone, quietly solve the problem, and come back with a solution.	In stressful times, women prefer to talk through a problem, verbalizing the many options in order to draw conclusions and come back with a solution.

Adapted from Elizabeth Pace, *The X and Y of Buy: Why Gender Matters in Sales and Marketing* (Thomas Nelson Publishing, 2009).

Coaching Across Career Cycle

As I wheeze up the rocky trail, I realize that I'm actually enjoying myself. I'm reminded of something that Lisa, an instructional coach in St. Joseph, Missouri, shared with me the week prior. She said, "You know, after being in this job for four years, it's finally starting to make sense. Everything connects. I finally feel like I see the big picture and now it's not as scary as it used to be." Today I'm having the same experience on my bike. The trails feel much more comfortable today and I haven't even had to pull out the map. After four years of riding these very same trails, they are starting to make sense to me and they are far less intimidating.

The next time I see Lisa, I mention the aha! I had on my mountain bike and she wonders aloud, "Is it something to do with having done this for four years now?" Neither of us are sure, but it leads me to wonder how level of experience impacts learning. Burden's work (1982) frames experience and career cycle according to the following stages:

1. *Survival Stage* (first year). Teachers are concerned about issues around classroom management; knowledge; and skills related to teaching the subject(s), improving their teaching skills, and making decisions about what to teach.

2. *Adjustment Stage* (second through fourth year). As teachers become more knowledgeable, they begin to see the complexities of teaching and learning and seek out support to meet a wider range of perceived needs. Generally, teachers become more relaxed and open as they feel they are more able to meet students' needs.

3. *Mature Stage* (fifth year and beyond). Teachers at this stage understand the teaching environment and feel more secure about their teaching. Many continue to try new teaching techniques in order to better meet the needs of the students.

Moving through these stages isn't guaranteed. While some teachers stagnate or leave the teaching profession before reaching the mature stage, others move through the stages with ease. Fessler (1995) believes that this is due to the *personal* and *organizational environments* of an individual. Examples of personal environment include life stage, family, personal milestones such as birth of children and marriage, interests and hobbies outside of the workplace, personal crisis, and individual dispositions and behaviors. Examples of organizational environment include management style of the school leader, professional organizations, regulations and processes related to accountability, and trust within the organization. He writes, "The teacher career cycle responds to environmental conditions. A supportive, nurturing, reinforcing environment can assist a teacher in the pursuit of a rewarding, positive career progression. Environmental interference and pressures, on the other hand, can impact negatively the career cycle" (p. 180).

Understanding both Burden's stages of the career cycle and Fessler's influences within the career cycle can help us design a differentiated model of professional development and coaching. Like coaching across generation and gender, addressing the needs related to career stages calls for a multifaceted and flexible approach that directly connects with adult learners where they are rather than where we may want them to be.

Coaching Across Processing Styles

As learners, we process information in different ways. In *Learning Along the Way* (2003), I introduced the work of Kenneth and Rita Dunn's processing styles: *global* and *analytic processors.*

> Global processors tend to be more random. They function better when goals are general and include multiple approaches and options. They work best in environments that offer background noise, music, and conversation, and prefer an informal agenda with opportunities for short breaks. Global processors also work best when tackling simultaneous projects. When putting together a piece of furniture a global processor might say, "I never read the directions because it takes too much time." (p. 55).

Analytic processors prefer working toward a clear set of objectives and are interested in reaching specific conclusions or outcomes. They appreciate a quiet environment and a formal agenda. Analytics tend to persist with few breaks and feel more comfortable tackling a single project at a time. An analytic might say, "I can't get anything done until I get organized."

Global and analytic processors approach all of life's tasks differently and need learning that adapts to their distinct needs. When it comes to professional development, global processors aren't happy when faced with successive teaching, a rigid and inflexible schedule, minimal peer activity, or listening for a long period of time. Analytics, on the other hand, become frustrated with humor and stories without objectives, too much noise or distraction, being forced into groups when they would rather work alone, and disorganized and unclear directions" (pp. 55–56).

Last week, I was working with a group of district-level coaches outside of Chicago. We broke ourselves into groups based on whether we were global or analytic learners. After having done this exercise with many groups, I wasn't surprised when it turned out that most of the group was analytic (about three quarters) and the rest were global. We discussed how the two groups affect each other by sharing (1) the things that drive us crazy about working with the other group and (2) what we'd like the other group to understand about us. You probably guessed that this was a rather lively discussion in which the analytics shared their need for working through a problem in a step-by-step fashion and their love for making lists. And the globals shared their preference for jumping into a problem and solving it as they went. The bottom line is, yet again, we have groups within our schools that go about their work in very different ways. All of these differences make a person wonder how on earth we will ever succeed in creating a collaborative school culture!

Meanwhile . . . in the Principal's Office

As a result of No Child Left Behind, nearly every school is under pressure to show measurable improvement among students. This begs the question of how a school leader can effectively influence teachers to take advantage of, and grow from, professional development. Should a principal require all teachers to participate? Should we view coaching as voluntary and allow teachers to opt in at their own discretion? Should we assign coaching to teachers who are struggling or are on a plan for improvement? And if we do take such an approach, what are the ramifications on the school culture? Wouldn't it be easy if we could mandate change and sit back and watch it happen? Unfortunately, that will never happen. The first step for principals is developing an understanding of adult learners so that principals can differentiate their approach and move all teachers along a learning continuum (Figure 8.4).

Thinking in terms of the adult learning continuum allows principals to recognize the hiccups that come with learning and address them. Instead of mandating change, savvy principals understand the importance of holding teachers accountable for certain things and presenting options for how teachers can get there. This is particularly effective in schools with well-developed systems for professional development that include opportunities for large-group learning, small-group collaboration, and one-on-one coaching. With a professional development system in place, principals are in a better position to require teachers to participate in some forms of professional development, like grade-level or department meetings, while also allowing teachers choice in how they engage in other forms of professional development, such as one-on-one coaching.

The nuances of how coaching is framed by the principal makes an enormous impact on the coach's interactions with teachers. When a principal understands that the coach is a *resource* rather than a person who is there to *fix* teachers, they can frame coaching in a positive way that may settle any fears that teachers have. When a principal believes that coaching is the answer to every problem in a school and frames

Figure 8.4   Adult Learning Continuum

Stage	Learner's Language	Options for Support at This Stage	Challenges at This Stage
Gaining an Awareness of the New Learning	• "What is this about?" • "How does it match what I already know?"	• Most of this stage can be addressed in small or large groups. • Give teachers time to think about the "why" and make the "why" student centered. • Provide models of new learning through video or classroom observation. • Create conversations for teachers about the new learning. • Engage in professional reading and discussion. • Validate what the teachers are already doing that applies to the new learning.	• Adult learners are often rebellious when something new is introduced. • There might be the feeling of "what I've done in the past isn't good enough." • The new learning might be looked at myopically and be disconnected from the teachers' previous work.
Analyzing New Ideas	• "How does this match what I believe about instruction?" • "Do I agree with this?" • "Why should I do this?"	• Most of this stage can be addressed in small or large groups. • Provide ample opportunities for teachers to sift through the new learning. • Make connections to the teachers' established practices. • Encourage teachers to voice their disagreements.	• Teachers who disagree can be intimidating. Be careful not to send verbal or nonverbal cues that their ideas aren't acceptable.
Deciding Whether to Engage in the New Learning	• "Do I want to fully engage, find out more, or keep my distance?"	• Most of this stage can be addressed in small or large groups. • Provide flexibility in how teachers adopt the new practices. • Hold teachers accountable for what they say they'll do. • Be understanding of the slower adopters.	• This can also be an intimidating stage. Think about these forms of agreement to frame your work: - I agree wholeheartedly with the new learning - I agree with the following reservations - I do not agree, and why

Seeking Out Places to Make Changes in Practice	• "Where can I apply what I'm learning?"	• Provide one-on-one coaching for this stage as teachers need individualized support to figure out where to apply the new practices within the context of what they are already doing. • Ongoing discussion with teams or grade levels supports the application of new ideas.	• This stage requires you to know a lot about the teacher and students. Spend time in the classroom before making any suggestions about where to make changes in practice. • This takes time and requires planning sessions, work in the classroom, and debriefing on a regular basis.
Overgeneralizing New Learning	• "I just want to try it, then I'll figure out what works."	• This part of the process can be messy. • Encourage the teacher to reflect on how the application is meeting the students' needs. • Provide the expectation that this is a work in progress. • Most of this stage depends on one-on-one coaching and some group discussion.	• This stage also requires planning sessions, work in the classroom, and debriefing on a regular basis. • The coach recognizes how the teacher is applying the new learning and manages the process of redirecting the teacher when necessary.
Applying the New Learning Effectively	• "I know just where this makes sense and now its working."	• Encourage teachers to share where they are in the process and what's working with their students. • Continue to provide one-on-one coaching and opportunities for group discussion.	• By now the teacher is implementing the new learning and will most likely continue to have questions. It's getting easier for the coach.
Applying the Learning to Other Situations	• "Now that I'm committed to this, how can I continue to develop in this area?"	• Assess student learning in relationship to the new learning. How did this benefit the students? • Continually "look back" to see where the learning has evolved from and to. • Plan next steps with teachers.	• Assessing the impact of the new learning on students is essential as it provides the most important "why" for the work. • Learning is recursive, "When we are done, we've just begun."

coaching as a hammer to hold teachers accountable, the coach will likely gain little traction.

Learning is about stepping out of the known and into the unknown, and coaches depend on the principal to put pressure on teachers through a clearly articulated vision. With a clear and well-understood vision, coaches can easily slip in and provide support to teachers. Without one, coaches often feel that they are only able to work with pockets of teachers who would probably do it anyway.

Tools and Techniques

Student-Centered Coaching Rubric: Understanding the Adult Learner

The following rubric is a guide for principals and coaches to reflect on their progress in working with adult learners.

Figure 8.5   Student-Centered Coaching Rubric

Trait: Understands How to Work With Adult Learners			
	Accomplished	*Developing*	*Novice*
The coach . . .	The coach has a well-formed understanding of adult learning research and flexibly adapts the coaching based on this knowledge to move the adult learning forward.	The coach has taken specific measures to develop an understanding of adult learning. The coach is more able to pinpoint and remedy problems when working with teachers.	The coach has little knowledge in adult learning research and has a hard time pinpointing the cause of problems when working with teachers.
The school leader . . .	The principal understands adult learners and creates a safe environment in which adults can take risks as learners. The principal has established a clear vision and teachers understand what is expected of them.	The principal is growing more adaptable to the adult learners in the school. There is more evidence of teachers taking risks as learners. The principal is honing the school vision and is more comfortable holding teachers accountable for certain practices.	The principal takes a passive approach or mandates change and expects the coach to hold teachers accountable to implement the change. There is confusion among teachers regarding what is expected of them.

Note: Please see the Resources for the complete rubric.

Understanding Generational Patterns Among Individuals

A frank conversation about how teachers view themselves and how they prefer to engage with others is a step in bridging the generational divide. So why do we so often charge ahead and assume that everyone looks at things the same way we do? These questions uncover generational influences among teachers.

Figure 8.6 Surveying Generational Patterns

1. What is your teaching history? When did you become a teacher?
2. Why did you become a teacher? What has kept you in the profession?
3. What do you find to be the most comforting aspects of your work?
4. Can you name an example of a time you were less comfortable at work?
5. How do you feel about collaboration with other teachers?
6. In what situations do you like to collaborate and when do you prefer to work on your own?
7. What do you want me to be sure I do as your coach?

Understanding Generational Patterns Among Groups

Another approach is to tackle generational conflict head on. The following activity helps teachers name and come to terms with their generational differences and take steps to move beyond any divides that may exist.

Figure 8.7 Talking About My (and Your) Generation

1. Form small groups using the following categories:
   o Traditionalists: Born before 1945
   o Baby Boomers: Born between 1946 and 1964
   o Generation X: Born between 1965 and 1980
   o Millennials: Born after 1980
2. Each generational group begins by charting important trends, icons, and events that have influenced their generation. Be sure to discuss the implications for this shared history. For example, Baby Boomers might chart how the Beatles influenced them (approximately 25 minutes).
3. Next, each generational group charts their perceptions, stereotypes, and general impressions of the other generational groups they work alongside (approximately 25 minutes).
4. Groups share both charts using the following questions (approximately 15 minutes):
   o What stereotypes or misconceptions arose from the discussion?
   o In what ways do the groups have a clearer understanding of each other as a result of the discussion?
   o How will this conversation influence our work together?

A Final Thought

I really don't think I would follow Cyndy up that big hill if I didn't trust her. Deep down, I know that she knows me and wouldn't put me in a position that I couldn't recover from. Though I know it means I have to take a risk, I also know that I may have a really good time.

Coaches can create the same conditions in their work with teachers. A primary theme of this chapter has been deepening our knowledge of what drives the behavior of adults as they face the risk that comes with new learning. We ask teachers to continue to push themselves in new directions on a daily basis, much like Cyndy challenges me on the trails. Yet we are surprised when we experience reluctance among teachers. It is our job to help others see the possible joy that comes with new learning and feel comfortable enough to bottle up our fears, or as Carl Jung once wrote, "The trouble is, if you don't risk anything, you risk everything."

9

Developing Systems and Structures to Support Coaches

Any coach will tell you that the shift from teaching to coaching is dramatic. Some coaches are lonely and miss the close connections they had with students. Others are in roles that are poorly articulated. Some are not prepared for the complexities of working with adult learners. And others face school cultures that are downright hostile to coaching. To meet these challenges, coaches require ongoing support that provides them with the opportunity to learn alongside a group of peers. This chapter draws upon my experience supporting coaches in a variety of districts and provides ideas for designing high-quality professional development to directly address their unique needs.

We can draw upon what we know about good instruction to differentiate support for coaches. The Parkway School District, just outside of St. Louis, began their coaching effort with a small team of three coaches. A team that became quite close as they transitioned into their new role with support from Lisa, their district-level leader. When year two came along, coaching was expanded to include an additional fifteen coaches, and Lisa was worried. She wasn't sure how to continue to support the original team of "veterans," create community across the whole team, and support the new coaches in their early stages of development. It was year two, and Lisa realized she had to differentiate to meet the needs of the coaching team. To accomplish this, we worked together to develop a model for supporting the Parkway coaches that included the following components:

Professional Development Focused on Coaching Practice (for the Full Coaching Team)

These sessions occurred four times across the year and were designed to build community and develop a shared understanding of the practices for student-centered coaching. Two times in the year, we included principals to ensure the messages about coaching were clear and consistent throughout the system. Topics included getting student-centered coaching up and running, scheduling and documenting the impact of coaching, using student evidence and student assessment data, incorporating theories of adult learning, managing change, and working with the principal to foster a learning-oriented school culture.

Professional Development Focused on Curriculum and Instruction (for the Full Coaching Team)

The Parkway coaches were simultaneously engaged in the development of a districtwide literacy curriculum for grades K–6. They came together regularly to analyze the literacy standards and engage in a process of backward design to develop the new district curriculum. At times, though, this created questions about the coach's role, such as are the coaches expected to hold teachers accountable for the literacy curriculum or is that the principal's job? How can they use the assessment tools that are built into the curriculum to propel their coaching? And what if schools aren't using the curriculum at all; what is the coach's job then? These questions led to rigorous dialogue among the coaching team that furthered the definition of their coaching role and helped them develop a deeper understanding of the literacy practices that were expected.

Small-Group Coaching Observations (for Five to Ten Coaches)

One of the most intensive forms of support for the Parkway coaches were coaching observations that were hosted by volunteers from the team and occurred four times a year. The observations focused on the typical work that coaches were engaged in, such as using student work with individual teachers or teams of teachers, working collaboratively with the principal, creating agreements with teachers, framing a focus for the coaching cycle, and having conversations about data. (Coaching observations are described in greater detail later in this chapter.)

One-On-One Coaching (With an Individual Coach)

Just like teachers, coaches benefit from the encouragement and support that is provided through one-on-one coaching. In Parkway, the newest members of the team were given priority for one-on-one sessions to help them develop as coaches. On a visit in the fall, I spent a few hours with Cartelia. As a new coach early in the school year, she was trying to navigate the school culture and make inroads with teachers. In our conversation, we discussed the dynamics of each grade-level team and brainstormed a few coaching moves that would meet teachers where they were and help them move forward. We also thought together about the School Improvement Plan to be sure that Cartelia's work was in alignment. Finally, we talked through some ideas to help Cartelia continue to build relationships and further define her role as a coach. Through our individualized conversation, I was able to meet her needs more directly than we could have done in a group session.

A Curriculum for Supporting New Coaches

Like the seasons, new coaches move through a series of predictable stages in their development across the first year. In the first few weeks of school, coaches are full of enthusiasm and *hopefulness* about the impact they will make with both students and teachers. And just about when the leaves begin to turn and fall from the trees, many coaches begin to feel *hopeless*. I have learned that when I meet with teams of new coaches in October, I'd better bring along the Kleenex. My theory is that this is the time when new coaches begin to realize the complexity of their new job, grow increasingly overwhelmed, and wonder why they decided to leave the classroom.

It benefits coaches to receive support that aligns with where they are in the process of becoming a coach. The following table describes a typical year at a glance for new coaches and can serve as a useful tool for developing a curriculum of coaching support (Figure 9.1).

Figure 9.1 Supporting New Coaches: A Year at a Glance

	Common Challenges for New Coaches	Support for New Coaches
Fall: August Through November	Early in the year, most new coaches are transitioning away from the classroom, and often worry about how to most effectively spend their time. October is the toughest month for new coaches, as they gradually become more concerned regarding how to make an impact on student learning.	At this stage, new coaches benefit from collaborative learning and coaching observations. Topics can include the following: • Collaborating with the school leader • Fostering relationships with teachers • Engaging teachers to participate in the coaching • Creating openings for coaching through small-group collaboration • Using data and student work as the foundation for one-on-one and small-group coaching • Putting a schedule together for coaching cycles (individual and small group) • Measuring the impact of coaching on student learning
Winter: November Through February	By now, most coaches have an established schedule that commonly includes teachers who are the early adopters. Coaches recognize the need to develop strategies for gaining entry with teachers who have not yet engaged. This is a great time for coaches to focus on coaching cycles before their work is interrupted by the spring testing season.	At this stage, new coaches benefit from continued collaboration with their colleagues, coaching observations, and one-on-one problem-solving sessions. Topics can include the following: • Developing strategies for working with a broad range of adult learners • Connecting with teachers who haven't engaged in a coaching cycle • Redesigning the coach's schedule to accommodate these teachers • Continuing to refine coaching practices such as using student work
Spring: March Through May	The spring testing season arrives and this often throws off the coach's schedule. During this stage, coaches can focus on the grade levels that aren't tested and support the testing in the other grades.	At this stage, new coaches benefit from continued collaboration with colleagues, coaching observations, and one-on-one problem-solving sessions. Topics can include the following: • Reflecting on the use of the Results-Based Coaching Tool and how their coaching has impacted both student learning and teaching practice • Setting goals and planning for the next year

Coaching Labs

In Chapter 6, you read about the value of observations, or learning labs, for teachers. In my work with districts, I've found that coaches also benefit from learning labs that are focused on coaching practice and write,

> Coaching labs provide coaches with the opportunity to meet with a small group of colleagues and observe a fellow coach who acts as a lab host. The goal of the labs is to provide coaches with time to observe one another's practice, as well as time for rigorous reflection. Participating coaches walk away with new ideas and tools for their own work and are able to take time in their busy professional lives to reflect. (Sweeney, 2007, p. 38)

Today's coaching lab will be hosted by Kimberly (a second-year coach) and will include Theresa, a fourth-grade teacher. They are joined by six observing coaches from the same district who are fairly new to the coaching role. By sitting in on their conversation, the coaching team will benefit from seeing how they work together to plan and deliver instruction.

A few weeks earlier, Kimberly and I met to plan the lab. As the facilitator, I wanted to be sure she understood the purpose, process, and protocol for the observation so she would feel comfortable and supported. I also shared that it was important to ground the observation in an authentic set of goals that she has for her coaching, or her "coaching look for's," and explained that we'd figure those out together and add them to the protocol so the observers would know what to focus on during the observation.

After some discussion, Kimberly pinpointed a set of coaching look for's that she had been thinking about since our last session. She explained that she was looking at her role differently now and didn't want to plow through the curriculum with teachers, but instead wanted to use student work as a guide for what to teach and use the curriculum as a resource. This has been challenging for her, and I commended her for focusing the coaching lab on an area where she has more questions than answers. She let me know that she also hoped to try out a new tool that the grade-level teams had been discussing to differentiate instruction, which they called the Four-Square Student Organizer (Figure 9.3). She hadn't used it yet and thought it might really fit with her goals for today. If it did work, she hoped that Theresa would share how it went with the rest of the team at a later date. We end up with the following look for's for Kimberly's observation:

- Our decisions will be based on the student work in conjunction with the literacy curriculum.
- My questions will connect the student work with instruction, such as "What are we seeing that needs to be addressed with the students?" "How will we address this need?"
- We will use the Four-Square Student Organizer to differentiate student learning.

I check to make sure Kimberly feels ready for the observation, and she says, "You know, I really feel fine about it, especially now that I've seen the protocol. My team is so supportive and professional and, to be honest, I think I will benefit the most because these are areas I've been trying to figure out for the past several weeks. I just hope that my focus benefits everyone else in the group." This is a common concern among coaches who host observations, and I ensure her that her focus will readily transfer to the work of her teammates, and they too will find that the conversation helps them think through areas they'd like to develop.

Moving Through a Coaching Observation

Participants in coaching labs benefit from a well-understood protocol and process. With such a process in place, the participants better understand the focus for the observation as well as the expected behaviors. This knowledge provides both structure and depth to the observation process. Figure 9.2 details the protocol we used when observing Kimberly and Theresa.

Figure 9.2 Protocol for Kimberly and Theresa's Coaching Lab

(Suggested time: 3.5 hours)

Coaching Look For's:

- Our decisions will be based on the student work in conjunction with the literacy curriculum.
- My questions will connect the student work with instruction, such as "What are we seeing that needs to be addressed with the students?" "How will we address this need?"
- We will use the Four-Square Student Organizer to differentiate student learning.

Setting the Context *30 minutes*	Participants learn about the professional development that is currently taking place in the school. The coach shares background, including previous work with this teacher and the goals for the coaching conversation. Participants are encouraged to ask clarifying questions.
Observe the Prebrief With the Teacher *15 minutes*	The group observes as the teacher and coach revisit their plan for the lesson. While observing, participants take notes that are specific to the coaching look for's.
Observe the Classroom Instruction *50 minutes*	The group observes the instruction and are given options for their note taking, such as • practice collecting student evidence that relates to the goals for student learning, and • observe the roles of the coach and teacher while in the classroom.
Observe the Debrief With the Teacher *40 minutes*	The group observes as the teacher and coach debrief the lesson. While observing, participants take notes that are specific to the look for's.

Debrief the Coaching
60 minutes
	The group debriefs the coaching in the following rounds:
	
	• Round 1: *Coaching Moves*
	  ○ Each group member takes a turn describing what he or she saw during the observation using objective language, such as "I saw . . . ," "I heard . . . ," "I noticed . . . ."
	  ○ The host of the observation listens and takes notes.
	
	• Round 2: *Impact on Student Learning*
	  ○ Each group member takes a turn describing the impact of the coaching on the student learning.
	  ○ The host of the observation listens and takes notes.
	
	• Round 3: *Implications and Questions Related to Coaching*
	  ○ The host of the observation responds and answers any questions that may have arisen in the first two rounds.
	  ○ Group members and the host name implications and ask questions related to the coaching.
	
	• Round 4: Next Steps
	  ○ Each group member and the host state a next step that arose from the observation. The facilitator takes notes for future support.

Setting the Context

Since some of the coaches in our group aren't familiar with Kimberly's school, we begin the observation with Kimberly providing background about how her work has been looking with the teacher who will participate today.

She explains that Theresa is a fourth-grade teacher with three years of teaching experience. She has always taught in the school and is reflective and very willing to participate in coaching. They are in the midst of a multiweek coaching cycle that is focused on nonfiction writing and are planning a lesson that they will co-teach later in the day. They began the coaching cycle at the beginning of the writing unit, and so far, Kimberly has spent two days a week in the classroom during writing time, along with a weekly planning session with Theresa.

Marsha, one of the observing coaches, asks, "Is this what most of your coaching is looking like? Or is Theresa the exception?"

Kimberly responds, "That's a great question. I'd say that she is one of the more willing teachers. There are others whom I haven't been able to connect with and I'm wondering how to get in with those people." I want to be careful to keep the observation focused on Kimberly's look for's and suggest that we talk more about engaging reluctant teachers at a later time and shift the conversation back to today's focus.

Kimberly describes that she is trying to focus her coaching on student work in conjunction with the literacy curriculum. In the past, she took teachers through the curriculum without analyzing the students' learning, and she is trying to shift more toward using the curriculum as a resource. With this teacher, she has noticed some students may not be getting the support they need when it comes to writing projects, and she wants to try using an organizer to help her differentiate more intentionally. As she shares her coaching look for's, I encourage the group to ask clarifying questions so they have a firm understanding of what they are there to observe.

Before wrapping up the prebriefing session, we read through and discuss the protocol and I share a few guidelines for the period of time that we'll be in the classroom (see Tools and Techniques at the end of this chapter).

Observing the Prebrief With the Teacher

A few minutes later, Theresa joins us. She and Kimberly sit side by side with their notebooks open and a stack of student work piled between them. It's been a few days since Kimberly has been in the classroom, and she asks, "How have the past few days gone? What are you noticing with your students?"

Theresa shares, "Now that we are a few weeks into the unit, I'm starting to run into the challenges I always have with writer's workshop . . . my students are at so many different places in their writing and I'm having a hard time reaching all of them."

Kimberly replies, "I've experienced the same problem. Let's think for a minute about where you would like the students to be right now with their projects, and then we can plan from that point."

Kimberly remembers that she wants to make decisions that are based in student work and quickly adds, "What if we look at a few of their notebooks to see where they are?"

They pick up Colby's notebook and read through it, and Theresa says, "Let's see. Colby is writing about the *Titanic*. He has made entries in his notebook that tie to the mini-lessons I've taught. Here I see (1) facts about the *Titanic*, (2) stories of people on the *Titanic*, 3) visual descriptions about the *Titanic*, (4) sensory descriptions about the *Titanic*, and (5) events related to the *Titanic*. Colby definitely is moving along through the project as I'd hoped. Can we compare his notebook to some others?" They agree and look together through several of the students' notebooks and confirm that some students, like Colby, have a lot of volume in their notebooks while others have very little. This, they agree, is essential for students to move on to the next phase of the project.

Kimberly listens carefully and restates what they have discussed so far, "So when it comes to the volume of ideas and writing in their notebooks, students are in different places so some of them will have a hard time moving into the actual reports."

"Exactly!" says Theresa.

Kimberly suggests they do a midunit assessment on volume and the quality of writing that students have so far, and then they'll be able to determine which students need more support, and they can problem-solve what to do with those students. Kimberly asks, "What if we make a quick checklist with indicators for what we want to see the students doing? It can include

- volume of entries that are based on the topic that they've selected;
- a variety of types of entries about the topic that connect to the mini-lessons, such as facts, visual descriptions, sensory descriptions, leads, and stories of people from the times; and
- notebook is organized and legible.

Theresa says, "These work but I wonder how many pages we should expect to see that are based on their topic. Do you think we could say five to ten pages in their notebooks?"

"I don't see why not; that seems like a good goal because with five to ten pages they will have enough material to work with when they go to write their final report," replies Kimberly.

"And hopefully a large amount of the writing will be used in their reports so that will make it easier for them later," adds Theresa. This part of the process was important because the writing curriculum involved the use of writer's notebooks as a place to collect writing ideas, practice writing techniques, and plan writing projects. They knew that if the students didn't have enough of this work done, they would be at a deficit when they moved forward to pull together their final reports.

They shift to a discussion about their roles for collecting student evidence. "Since it's hard to get around to all the kids, what if during today's lesson, I focus on collecting student evidence while you teach?" suggests Kimberly.

"That's a great idea. I was planning to teach a mini-lesson on leads and the students are going to write several leads in their notebooks. It would be really helpful for you to observe the students to see what they do during writing time. Are they writing leads? Are they sitting there stuck? What else is in their notebooks? I just can't get around to all of them, so if you helped me to know what's going on with the full class, I might be able to figure out what to do next."

Kimberly agrees and adds, "This will give us a lot of evidence and then we'll be able to do some differentiating. That reminds me, what if we use the Four-Square Student Organizer that we've talked about in our team meetings as a tool for grouping kids when we meet after the lesson?"

Theresa agrees and says, "I think that would really help, then maybe I can plan some small-group instruction based on what we find." As the conversation between Kimberly and Theresa unfolds, the observing coaches busily take notes, trying to capture every detail of the conversation.

Observing the Classroom Instruction

As Kimberly and Theresa move through the lesson, the coaches are spread throughout the classroom scribbling notes. They watch as the teacher and coach work in tandem to provide instruction while simultaneously collecting relevant student evidence. The lesson wraps up, and Theresa grabs a pile of writer's notebooks to bring to the debriefing session that follows.

Observing the Debrief With the Teacher

The observing coaches barely have the chance to settle into their chairs as Theresa is already asking Kimberly, "What did you see? I'm dying to know."

Kimberly wonders, "Should we talk first about what I saw or start by looking at the notebooks?"

Theresa thinks for a minute, "That's a good point, let's start with the notebooks and then we can talk about what you saw after that."

They page through each of the students' writer's notebooks and compare them to the checklist they created in the prebriefing session. They agree to make three piles: exceeding the standard on the checklist, meeting the standard, and below the standard. Since the checklist is clear and straightforward, this part of the conversation doesn't take long. They end up with eleven students who are exceeding, nine who are meeting, and four who are below. Theresa says, "I'm relieved. This helps me see that most of my class is ready to move on in the writing project and I have a small group that may need some intensive instruction, but I think we can get them there." Kimberly suggests they try adding some names to the Four-Square Student Organizer to figure out the next steps for instruction, and Theresa asks, "Well, I guess I'm wondering what you saw the students doing during writing time. This could help us decide what to focus on in the groups."

Kimberly turns to her notes and says, "Let's see, I noticed a large group of students, mostly the ones who are in the meeting or exceeding group, that have a lot written in their notebooks. I wonder . . . if we want them to continue adding volume in their notebooks, then we may need to provide them with some research strategies. Maybe we can partner with the librarian on that. Then another group are on the right track but they aren't organized and can't reread what they wrote. With them, we could do some quick small-group lessons on the importance of organizing and rereading what they have written in the writer's notebook to help with the final project." Theresa nods in agreement. "Then I noticed several students that just need to write a lot more before we can start their final projects. Michael is having a hard time staying focused and wandered around. Francie is really worried about spelling, which is slowing her down. And Marie—oh this was interesting . . . let's pull out her notebook." They sift through the pile and pull out Marie's notebook so they can take a closer look. "She isn't writing entries about her topic. She's writing the whole report in her notebook. This is making her struggle to use the crafting techniques that you are teaching in your mini-lessons. I think we just need to confer with her to redirect her about how to use her notebook." As they talk, Theresa adds the areas of instructional focus and students' names to the Four-Square Student Organizer (Figure 9.3).

Figure 9.3   Kimberly and Theresa's Four-Square Student Organizer

Coaching Cycle Focus: Nonfiction Writing Projects	
Goals for Students: • Volume of entries that are based on the topic • A variety of types of entries about the topic that connect to the mini-lessons • Notebook is organized and legible	
Group 1 Instructional Goal: Techniques for using research to add more to their writer's notebooks. Colby Collin Luz Anna Margo Jake S. Spencer Madison Thomas Mica Ava Haley Conner	**Group 2 Instructional Goal:** Being more organized so that what is in the notebook can be used later. Will Caroline Jake M.
Group 3 Instructional Goal: Writing more entries, increasing volume. Devon Anna H. Michael Ruthie	**Group 4 Instructional Goal:** Meet with Marie in a writing conference to talk about how to use the writer's notebook as a place to collect ideas to use in later writing. Go through her notebook and highlight the material that she is most interested in using in her final report.
Whole Class Instructional Needs Continue teaching mini-lessons to encourage more entries in the writer's notebooks that include techniques for research. In about a week, when Groups 2 and 3 have increased their volume, check the rubric again to see if it's time to begin writing the final reports.	

Note: See the Resources for a template of this tool.

When Kimberly and Theresa finish, they have a clear vision for next steps that are based on the student evidence. Theresa says, "I think I'll do some guided writing with Group 3. That way I can be right there with them to make sure they are moving along. I think Group 1 might be able to go down to the library and do some research if we help them with a few strategies. Marie needs a conference. And

Group 2, once they get their writing cleaned up, can join Group 1. This should only take a week or so and then everyone will be ready to move forward with their projects."

Kimberly listens, and then asks, "I'll be in your class a few times next week; how can I help?"

Theresa says, "I could use your help planning and co-teaching some lessons about researching. In fact, I think we should do that with the whole class. And would you sit in with me on the conference with Marie? And when I'm doing the other guided writing groups, it would be great if you could be in the class to manage the others."

Kimberly smiles and says, "That sounds like a great plan. Then, we might want to come back to the checklist we created today to see if more of the students are at meeting and exceeding. Then we'll know we are ready to move forward with the projects." They agree and Theresa races back to class, notebooks in her arms.

Debriefing the Coaching

After a short break, the coaches debrief the coaching that they observed. I begin this part of the conversation by restating Kimberly's coaching look for's:

- Our decisions will be based on the student work in conjunction with the literacy curriculum.
- My questions will connect the student work with instruction, such as "What are we seeing that needs to be addressed with the students?" "How will we address this need?"
- We will use the Four-Square Student Organizer to differentiate student learning.

I also remind the group that what we are looking for are evidence-based descriptions of what they observed and to refrain from sharing judgments or making suggestions about what Kimberly could have done differently. By being evidence based, we can ensure that coaching observations provide respect for the hosting coach and also move the conversation to a deep level of discourse and reflection.

We begin the first round with the coaches by sharing what they noticed, saw, and heard in the prebrief, classroom observation, and debrief. Mary Beth shares, "I noticed how important the checklist was to guide the conversation, yet how little time it took to create."

Marsha adds, "I saw the teacher and coach sitting side by side and looking at the student work to decide where kids were in relationship to the goals."

Mark shares, "I heard the coach clarifying what the teacher said. And I noticed a trusting relationship between the teacher and coach." While the group notes what they observed, Kimberly and I listen and take notes.

In round two, we discuss how the coaching conversation will impact the students in Theresa's classroom. Shawna says, "The role that the coach played during the instructional time helped to make sure no students fell through the cracks. For example, noticing how Marie was using her notebook. This will help that student get what she needs to be successful."

Laura says, "Using the Four-Square Organizer made it very concrete. This will increase student achievement because the teacher has a specific plan for each student. "

Amy nods and adds, "Pairing the student work with the checklist and the organizer made it all come together. And it's all based on what the students need. Theresa is going to be able to deliver some very targeted instruction thanks to that planning session."

We move into the third round by hearing some thoughts from Kimberly. She shares that she now feels more comfortable using student work and that it is becoming more natural the more she does it. She sees that she can still really address curriculum while also analyzing the students' needs. She also liked the Four-Square Student Organizer and has another teacher she plans to try it out with. She's also planning to ask Theresa to share how it worked with the rest of her team. She comes back to her earlier question about how to encourage some of the more reluctant teachers to participate in this type of coaching and thinks they would find it helpful if they would just give it a chance. Since Theresa is a leader at her grade level, Kimberly wants to think more about how to get some sharing happening about their coaching cycle with the other teachers.

We move on to discuss other implications for our coaching, and Laura says, "I really see the value of the student work. This is so important and I want to do more of it."

Shawna adds, "And it verifies the importance of coaching cycles . . . it requires the coach to be in the classroom, working with the kids, over a period of time." Mark shares that he too would like to think about how to do this type of work with teachers who are less engaged in coaching. And Mary Beth wants to be more focused in coaching conversations and thinks that the checklist was a key element for maintaining that focus.

I close the session by asking each of the coaches to share a next step for their work with teachers. We also agree as a group to further explore the question of working with less engaged teachers. As we wrap up, the coaches express their gratitude for the opportunity to explore coaching in such a deep and thought-provoking way. They liked the protocol and hope we'll do more of these observations. Mark summed it up with, "I never get the chance to see how other coaches work with teachers. I really appreciate this opportunity to expand as a coach."

Meanwhile . . . in the District Office

Leading a coaching effort inevitably presents questions about which types of support to provide. District leaders strive to find the right balance and develop systems and structures of support to help coaches be successful in their work with teachers and students. Roles for a district leader can include the following:

Keeping the Lines of Communication Open Between Coaches, Principals, and the District

Coaching is adversely affected when communication breaks down between coaches, principals, and the district. This is especially true when the different parties carry differing definitions of the coach's roles and responsibilities. Designing support that includes principals creates a fully functioning system for coaching.

Establishing the Expectation and Tools for Evaluating the Impact of Coaching

In Chapter 5, you learned about several tools that are used to evaluate the impact of coaching. When districts set forth the expectation to use methods like these, or others, to evaluate the impact of coaching, they provide a measure of accountability throughout the system. This protects coaches from the vulnerable position of not quantifying their impact on students, and serves to reinforce the important role they serve in our schools.

Managing Time and Support for Coaches

There is a constant tug and pull when it comes to removing coaches from their schools for their own professional development. As Lisa from Parkway School District puts it, "We have to give the coaches the support they need to sharpen their saws, but we can't do it at the expense of the teachers and students in their schools." As a district leader with big expectations for her coaching team, Lisa has to carefully think through her purpose for pulling coaches out of their schools and how often to do it. For example, when she designs an annual three-day retreat for the coaches, she struggles with what type of work to do that focuses on coaching practice, and how much to emphasize curriculum and instruction.

Facilitating Coaching Labs

Coaching labs are protocol based and require skilled facilitation to ensure that they encourage rigorous dialogue that is safe and secure for the hosting coach. It is also ideal for coaching labs to connect to other learning because it provides real-life examples of how the coaching model looks in action.

Facilitating coaching observations is a logical role for a district leader and involves knowledge and expertise in areas such as (1) leading objective conversations that are rooted in evidence, (2) keeping the group focused on the coaching look for's, (3) setting norms for observations, (4) listening and probing participants for specificity, (5) distilling implications for our coaching work, and (6) soliciting next steps from participants.

The structure of a protocol provides a focused and safe environment for coaches to take risks, and I never facilitate an observation without one. The protocol we used with Kimberly and Theresa is designed to peel away like the layers of an onion. As the participants move through the rounds, they gain deeper insight into what they observed and what the implications are for their coaching.

In advance of the observation, I meet with the coach to discuss (1) the type of coaching conversation we'll observe; (2) which teacher, or teachers, to include; (3) the focus and coaching look for's for the observation; and (4) whether we will spend time in the classroom. If the coach chooses not to include a classroom component, we use the modified protocol in Figure 9.4.

Figure 9.4 Modified Protocol for Coaching Observations Without a Classroom Visit

(Suggested time: 3 hours)	
Coaching Look For's:	
Understanding the Context *30 minutes*	Participants learn about the professional development that is currently taking place in the school. The coach shares background, including previous work with this teacher and the goals for the coaching conversation. Participants are encouraged to ask clarifying questions.

Observe the Coaching Conversation *40 minutes*	The group observes the coaching conversation. While observing, participants take notes that are specific to the coaching focus and look for's.

Debrief the Coaching *60 minutes*	The group debriefs the coaching in the following rounds:
	
	• Round 1: *Coaching Moves*
	  o Each group member takes a turn describing what he or she saw during the observation using objective language, such as "I saw . . . ," "I heard . . . ," and "I noticed . . . ."
	  o The host of the observation listens and takes notes.
	
	• Round 2: *Impact on Student Learning*
	  o Each group member takes a turn describing the impact of the coaching on the student learning.
	  o The host of the observation listens and takes notes.
	
	• Round 3: *Implications and Questions Related to Coaching*
	  o The host of the observation responds and answers any questions that may have arisen in the first two rounds.
	  o Group members and the host name implications and ask questions related to the coaching.
	
	• Round 4: *Next Steps*
	  o Each group member and the host state a next step that arose from the observation. The facilitator takes notes for future support.

Tools and Techniques

Guidelines for Coaching Observations

Some educators are rarely provided the opportunity to observe in other classrooms. Therefore, before bringing any group into a classroom, I orient them to the following guidelines.

- Silence is golden—honor the existing tone, structure, and community in the classroom. Side conversations are distracting and upset the carefully developed learning environment.
- Come with a positive attitude and be a learner—we are not here to critique the coach or teacher.
- Maintain focus—keep the coaching look for's in mind during the observation.
- Be ready to think through the entire process—the prebrief, the observation, and the debrief.
- Remember that you are a visitor in the classroom. Please do not engage with students unless that has been a clearly established

part of the process. Trust that the teacher knows the students and is a professional.

- Take notes—bringing your recorded observations back to the debriefing session raises the quality of the conversation.

Note-Taking Template

The following note-taking template (Figure 9.5) is simple and serves to reinforce the importance of staying cognizant of the coaching look for's while participating in a coaching observation. It also reminds participants of the importance of note taking during observations.

Figure 9.5   Note-Taking Template for Coaching Observations

Coaching Look For's:

Observations:

A Final Thought

Supporting a team of coaches isn't easy. It demands a vision that meets the requirements of the system while also addressing the needs of individuals. But by applying what we know about good instruction, we can better support coaches. What we can't do, however, is assume that they are smart people who can figure this out on their own. Taking this approach puts coaches in a lonely position and can disrupt the entire school system. By creating opportunities for coaches to learn together, we can create touchstone experiences that launch rigorous discussion about the work we do with teachers and garner greater results with students.

In Closing

It is my goal that this book supports educators at all levels to take a humanistic, individualized, *and* data-driven approach to school-based coaching. We have struggled in the past to combine these features, yet as our schools face increasing demands for innovation and change, we long for an approach that gets results while also respecting our teachers and students.

Though teaching can be seen as a technical endeavor, we can't risk looking at teachers as machines. They are individuals who bring a complex array of knowledge and experiences to their teaching lives. In the past, some forms of coaching have been more about "fixing" a teacher's deficiencies and less about cultivating learning. We have found that this approach doesn't take us very far and only serves to divide a school culture into those that are "doing it" and those that aren't.

In his work on learning organizations, Peter Senge argues that we can take a living systems approach to change versus a mechanical mindset. In an interview with Allan M. Webber, Senge says, "We keep bringing in mechanics—when what we need are gardeners. We keep trying to drive change—when what we need to do is cultivate change." He adds,

> A relationship with a machine is fundamentally a different kind of relationship: It is perfectly appropriate to feel that if it doesn't work, you should fix it. But we get into real trouble whenever we try to "fix" people. We know how to create and nurture close friendships or family relationships. But when we enter the realm of the organization, we're not sure which domain to invoke. Should we evoke the domain of the machine? After all, much of our daily life is about interacting with computers, tape recorders, automobiles, and ATMs. Or should we evoke the domain of living systems—because a lot of our daily life is about interacting with family, friends, and colleagues? It shifts profoundly how you think about leadership and change. If you use a machine lens, you get leaders who are trying to drive change through formal change programs. If you use a living-systems lens, you get leaders who approach change as if they were growing something, rather than just "changing" something. Even on a large scale, nature doesn't change things mechanically: You don't just pull out the old and replace it with the new. Something new grows, and it eventually supplants the old. (2007)

Margaret Wheatley concurs and writes,

> But this 21st century world of complexity and turbulence is no place for the mechanistic thinking of the past. We are confronted daily by events and outcomes that surprise us. Nothing moves slowly enough for us to make sense of the world using any analytic process we were taught. And the complexity of modern systems cannot be understood by separating issues into neat boxes and diagrams. In a complex system, it is impossible to find simple causes that explain our problems, or to know who to blame. A messy tangle of relationships has given rise to these unending crises. We need a different world view to guide us in this new world of continuous change and intimately connected systems that reach around the globe. (1999)

By combining data-driven coaching practices with a humanistic approach, we are driven by what matters . . . the success of each and every student, teacher, coach, and school leader in our schools. And isn't that what really matters?

Resource A

Tools for the Assessment and Evaluation of Coaching

Student-Centered Coaching Rubric

Trait: Understands and Implements Student-Centered Coaching			
	Accomplished	*Developing*	*Novice*
The coach . . .	Student learning directly and consistently informs coaching conversations. The coach seamlessly guides the conversation from student learning to other factors such as the implementation of a program or curriculum, and classroom routines.	The coach is beginning to draw on student data in coaching sessions. The coach is more capable in addressing other factors, such as the implementation of a program or curriculum, and classroom routines in the context of student learning.	The coach rarely draws from student data in coaching sessions. Coaching is consistently focused on teaching practice, implementation of a program or curriculum, or classroom routines.
The school leader . . .	The principal understands the core practices for student-centered coaching, subscribes to those practices, and provides support to move the coach's work forward. The principal provides the necessary pressure and support to the adult learners in the school.	The principal has some knowledge of the core practices for student-centered coaching or may question its value. The principal is beginning to find a balance between providing the adequate pressure and support to the adult learners in the school.	The principal is not supportive of, or lacks knowledge in the core practices for, student-centered coaching. The principal has not yet achieved a balance of providing pressure and support to the adult learners in the school.

(Continued)

(Continued)

Trait: Understands How to Work With Adult Learners			
	Accomplished	*Developing*	*Novice*
The coach . . .	The coach has a well-formed understanding of adult learning research and flexibly adapts the coaching based on this knowledge to move the adult learning forward.	The coach has taken specific measures to develop an understanding of adult learning. The coach is more able to pinpoint and remedy problems when working with teachers.	The coach has little knowledge in adult learning research and has a hard time pinpointing the cause of problems when working with teachers.
The school leader . . .	The principal understands adult learners and creates a safe environment in which adults can take risks as learners. The principal has established a clear vision and teachers understand what is expected of them.	The principal is growing more adaptable to the adult learners in the school. There is more evidence of teachers taking risks as learners. The principal is honing the school vision and is more comfortable holding teachers accountable for certain practices.	The principal takes a passive approach or mandates change and expects the coach to hold teachers accountable to implement the change. There is confusion among teachers regarding what is expected of them.
Trait: Knowledge of Effective Teaching Practices			
	Accomplished	*Developing*	*Novice*
The coach . . .	The coach has extensive experience in a broad range of grade levels and subject areas. The coach continues to broaden his or her experience in order to deepen the current knowledge base.	The coach has taken specific measures to broaden the range of teaching experience across a range of grade levels and subject areas. The coach is currently developing knowledge of the content that is being coached.	The coach is capable and experienced across a limited range of grade levels and subject areas. The coach is still gaining experience in the content that is being coached.
The school leader . . .	The school leader has a well-developed pedagogical understanding and is able to recognize and provide feedback to teachers in direct relationship to the expected teaching practices.	The school leader has a developing sense of pedagogy and may understand some areas of instruction better than others. The school leader is able to provide specific feedback in some areas but not all.	The school leader lacks pedagogical understanding and is therefore unable to provide teachers with specific expectations and feedback regarding instruction.

Trait: Relationship Building			
	Accomplished	*Developing*	*Novice*
The coach . . .	The coach works effectively with all teachers due to specific measures he or she has taken to build trusting and professional relationships.	The coach is beginning to build trusting relationships with a broader array of teachers, including more challenging teachers.	The coach is able to build trusting relationships with a limited group of teachers.
The school leader . . .	The school leader works effectively to build collegial relationships with teachers and also understands the importance of providing the coach with the time that it takes to build and sustain collegial relationships.	The school leader is working toward the development of collegial relationships with teachers, and struggles to provide the coach with the necessary support to build and sustain collegial relationships with teachers.	The school leader questions the role of relationships and collegiality in the school setting or may struggle personally to build collegial relationships with teachers.
Trait: Skilled Facilitation			
	Accomplished	*Developing*	*Novice*
The coach . . .	The coach understands which facilitation processes to employ at any given time. The coach is a skilled facilitator and, as a result, both small and large groups function in a highly productive manner on a consistent basis.	The coach is working to expand the repertoire of facilitation techniques used in small- and large-group sessions. Groups are beginning to function at a more productive level.	The coach employs a limited set of facilitation processes. Small- and/or large-group facilitation are not productive on a consistent basis.
The school leader . . .	The school leader also understands and employs facilitation processes that support group work.	The school leader is working to develop the necessary skills to support group work through facilitative processes.	The school leader is learning the skills related to leading group work.

(Continued)

(Continued)

Trait: Maintains a Learning Stance			
	Accomplished	*Developing*	*Novice*
The coach . . .	The coach consistently seeks new experiences and opportunities for learning rather than taking the stance of an "expert."	The coach takes advantage of some opportunities for new learning, and is becoming more comfortable regarding taking the stance of "co-learner" with teachers.	The coach does not take advantage of opportunities for new learning on a consistent basis, and does not take the stance of "co-learner" with teachers.
The school leader . . .	The school leader sets the tone that "we are all learners" and models this behavior as an individual.	The school leader is working toward developing transparency regarding his or her own learning and development.	The school leader reinforces the status quo rather than a learning environment.

Trait: Reflective Dialogue			
	Accomplished	*Developing*	*Novice*
The coach . . .	The coach encourages reflective dialogue by asking open-ended questions, probing, and using paraphrasing techniques rather than simply giving the teacher answers.	The coach is beginning to use strategies such as asking open-ended questions, probing, and paraphrasing techniques to encourage reflective dialogue among teachers.	The coach does not use conversational approaches that encourage reflective dialogue among teachers.
The school leader . . .	The school leader uses specific strategies to encourage reflective dialogue among teachers.	The school leader is working toward the development of a reflective school culture.	The school leader is beginning to develop strategies for encouraging teacher reflection.

Trait: Productive Relationship Between the Coach and School Leader			
	Accomplished	*Developing*	*Novice*
The coach . . .	The coach understands his or her appropriate role as a coach while also understanding how to work collaboratively with the school leader.	The coach and school leader are beginning to find better definition regarding their unique roles, and are working more collaboratively.	The coach and school leader do not work collaboratively. The coach is unclear regarding the coaching role and how it relates to the role of the school leader.

	Accomplished	*Developing*	*Novice*
The school leader . . .	The school leader fully understands and supports the implementation of student-centered coaching. Time is allocated for the coach and principal to meet on a regular basis.	The school leader is developing an understanding of student-centered coaching. The principal and coach meet informally to touch base, and support for the coach is less predictable and consistent.	The school leader is developing an understanding of student-centered coaching. The principal and coach do not meet together or work collaboratively.

Results-Based Coaching Tool

Teacher's Name:		Coach's Name:	

Coaching Cycle Focus:

Dates of Coaching Cycle:

_____ to _____
beginning date   ending date

What is the student learning goal for this coaching cycle? What data is this goal based on?	What instructional practices were determined by the coach and teacher to most likely produce the desired student learning goal?	What coaching practices were implemented during this coaching cycle? (check all that apply)	As a result of the coaching cycle, what instructional practices is the teacher now using on a consistent basis?	What is the evidence that students accomplished the desired learning goal?
Student Learning Goal: Standard: **Baseline Data:** _____ % of students were able to do _____ as determined by the _____ assessment. Number of Students_____		☐ Demonstration teaching with a prebrief, lesson, and debrief ☐ Co-teaching with a prebrief, lesson, and debrief ☐ Collaborative planning ☐ Analysis of student work ☐ Teacher observation with a prebrief, lesson, and debrief ☐ Study group to discuss professional text that aligns to the student learning goal ☐ Other:_____		**Postassessment Data:** _____ % of students were able to do _____ as determined by the _____ assessment.

Results-Based Coaching Tool for Small Groups

Teachers' Names:		Coach's Name:		
Purpose for the Group Work:		Dates of Small Group Coaching Cycle:		
What did we learn from analyzing the student work?	What is our goal for student learning?	How will we extend our learning as a group?	As a result of the small-group coaching cycle, what instructional practices are the teachers planning to use?	What is the evidence that students accomplished the desired learning goal?
What student work did we examine?	Student Learning Goal:	Text-Based Collaboration Problem-Based Collaboration Observation: Demonstration Observation: Peer-Based Video One-On-One Coaching More examination of student work Other:		Postassessment Data:
What did we find?				
Preassessment Data:				

Resource B

Agreements

Teacher and Coach Agreement

Section 1: Coaching Focus

- What do you hope students will learn as a result of our coaching work?
- Is there any student work or data that could help us decide on a focus that would make the most impact with students?

Section 2: Strategies for Coaching and Collaboration

- How would you like to interact during our time in the classroom (co-teach, model, observe)?
- I suggest a weekly planning session for 30–45 minutes; what time works for you?
- It is also important for me to be in your classroom for one to three times per week; what time is best for you based on your goal for students?
- How would you like to communicate between our planning sessions (meetings, e-mails, other)?

Section 3: Meeting the Teacher's Needs

- Do you have any other concerns about the coaching?
- Is there anything you want me to be sure to do as your coach?

Principal and Coach Agreement

I. THE WORK

On what topics/areas should we focus to improve student learning?

- How has or might student data inform this decision?
- If necessary, how will we gather the appropriate student data (student work samples, tests, etc.)?
- How will we collect data across time to demonstrate the impact of coaching on teacher and student learning?

II. DEFINING OUR ROLES

- What roles and responsibilities will we each have in leading professional development (large group, small group, and one-on-one)?

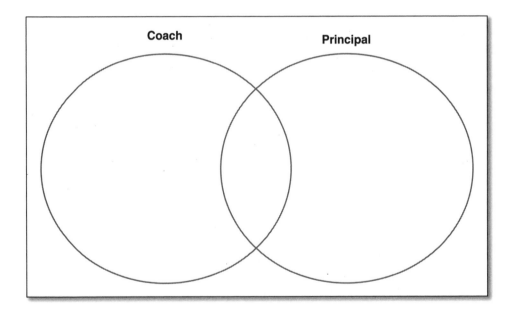

- How will we introduce the coaching role to the staff?

III. ONGOING COMMUNICATION AND SCHEDULING

- How and when will we communicate?
- What will the coach's schedule look like?
- How will we support each other?

Resource C

Tools for Note Taking and Documentation

Note-Taking Tool for Student-Centered Labs

Teacher:		
Facilitator:		
School:		
Date:		
Focus		
Look For's		
	Student Evidence	Instructional Practices

(Continued)

(Continued)

Next Steps for Instruction & Assessment	
Lingering Questions & Support Needed	

Student-Centered Teacher Evaluation Form

Teacher Name	Observer Name
Grade/Subject	School
Pre Conference Date	Time
Observation Date	Time
Post Conference Date	Time

Pre Conference

1. What are your goals for the students during the time in which you will be observed?

2. What have you done in the past that relates to this goal?

3. How does the goal connect to the standards and curriculum for your grade/subject?

4. What do you expect to see students doing in relationship to the goal?

5. Will you provide any individuals or groups of students with extra assistance (ELL, special education, etc.)? If so, how?

6. Do you have any students who may need other forms of instruction (i.e., gifted, etc.)?

7. How would you like me to collect student evidence during the observation?

Observation

Observations of Student Learning

Observations of Teacher Practice

Post Conference

1. What was observed that provides evidence of student learning that relates to the teacher's goal?

2. What was observed that indicated the need for follow-up by the teacher?

3. In what ways did the teaching practice move student learning forward?

4. What was observed that indicated the need for further development of teacher practice?

5. What resources is the school prepared to provide to support the development of teacher practice?

Resource D

Books and Journals to Support
Student-Centered Coaching

Websites and Journals That
Support Coaches and Principals

Student-Centered Coaching—www.studentcenteredcoaching.ning.com
Spark Innovation—www.sparkinnovate.com
Choice Literacy—www.choiceliteracy.com
Educational Leadership—www.ascd.org
Journal of Staff Development—www.nsdc.org
Literacy Coaching Clearinghouse—www.literacycoachingonline.org

Coaching

Burkins, J. M. (2007). *Coaching for balance: How to meet the challenges of literacy coaching.* Newark, DE: International Reading Association.

Dozier, C. (2006). *Responsive literacy coaching: Tools for creating and sustaining purposeful change.* Stenhouse: Portland, ME.

Flaherty, J. (1999). *Coaching: Evoking excellence in others.* Boston, MA: Butterworth-Heinemann.

Frost, S., Buhle, R., & Blachowicz, C. (2009). *Effective literacy coaching.* Alexandria, VA: ASCD.

Killion, J., & Harrison, C. (2006). *Taking the lead: New roles for teachers and school-based coaches.* Oxford, OH: NSDC.

Knight, J. (2009). *Coaching: Approaches and perspectives.* Thousand Oaks, CA: Corwin.

Knight, J. (2007). *Instructional coaching: A partnership approach to improving instruction.* Thousand Oaks, CA: Corwin.

Neufeld, B., & Roper, D. (2003). *Coaching: A strategy for developing instructional capacity: Promises and practicalities.* Washington, DC: Aspen Institute Program on Education and the Annenberg Institute for School Reform.

Sadder, M., & Nidus, G. (2009). *The literacy coach's game plan: Making teacher collaboration, student learning, and school improvement a reality.* Newark, DE: International Reading Association.

Toll, C. (2006). *Literacy coach's desk reference: The processes and perspectives for effective coaching.* Urbana, IL: National Council of Teachers of English.

Toll, C. (2005). *The literacy coach's survival guide: Essential questions and practical answers.* Newark, DE: International Reading Association.

Culture, Climate, and Change

Bridges, W. (1991). *Transitions: Making sense of life's changes* (2nd ed.). Cambridge, MA: Perseus Books Group.

Evans, R. (1996). *The human side of school change: Reform, resistance, and the real-life problems of innovation.* San Francisco, CA: Jossey-Bass.

Fullan, M. (2001). *Leading in a culture of change.* San Francisco, CA: Jossey-Bass.

Muhammad, A. (2009). *Transforming school culture.* Bloomington, IN: Solution Tree Press.

Wiggins, G., & McTighe, J. (2005). *Understanding by design.* Alexandria, VA: ASCD.

Gender and Generational Research

Lancaster, L. C., & Stillman, D. (2002). *When generations collide.* New York, NY: Harper Business.

Lovely, S., & Buffum, A. (2007). *Generations at school: Building an age-friendly learning community.* Thousand Oaks, CA: Corwin.

Pace, E. (2009). *The X and Y of buy.* Nashville, TN: Thomas Nelson.

Leadership and Learning

Allen, J. (2006). *Becoming a literacy leader: Supporting learning and change.* Portland, ME: Stenhouse.

Harwayne, S. (1999). *Going public: Priorities and practices at the Manhattan New School.* Portsmouth, NH: Heinemann.

Marzano, R. J., & Waters, T. (2009). *District leadership that works: Striking the right balance.* Bloomington, IN: Solution Tree Press.

Senge, P. (2000). *Schools that learn.* New York, NY: Doubleday Press.

Wheatley, M. (2002). *Turning to one another.* San Francisco, CA: Berrett-Koehler.

Wiggins, G., & McTighe, J. (2005). *Understanding by design.* Alexandria, VA: ASCD.

Professional Development

City, E. A., Elmore, R. F., Fiarman, S. E., & Teitel, L. (2009). *Instructional rounds in education.* Cambridge, MA: Harvard Education Press.

DuFour, R., Eaker, R., & DuFour, R. (2005). *On common ground: The power of professional learning communities.* Bloomington, IN: NES.

DuFour, R., & Eaker, R. (1998). *Professional learning communities at work: Best practices for enhancing student achievement.* Bloomington, IN: NES.

Guskey, T., & Huberman, M. (Eds.). (1995). *Professional development in education.* New York, NY: Teachers College Press.

Killion, J. (2008). *Assessing impact: Evaluating staff development.* Thousand Oaks, CA: Corwin.

Sweeney, D. (2003). *Learning along the way: Professional development by and for teachers.* Portland, ME: Stenhouse.

References

Armstrong, J. (1998). *Shipwreck at the bottom of the world: The extraordinary true story of Shackleton and the Endurance.* New York: Random House.

Barth, R. (1995). *Professional development in education.* New York: Teachers College Press.

Barth, R. (2006). Improving relationships in the schoolhouse. *Educational Leadership, 66*(6), 8–13.

Barth, R. (2007). *Educational leadership.* San Francisco, CA: Jossey-Bass.

Bridges, W. (1991). *Transitions: Making sense of life's changes* (2nd ed.). Cambridge, MA: Perseus Books Group.

Burden, P. (1982). *Developmental supervision: Reducing teacher stress at different career stages.* Paper presented at the Annual Meeting of the Association of Teacher Educators, Phoenix, AZ.

Christman, J., Ruth, B., Neild, C., Bulkley, K., Blanc, S., Liu, R., Mitchell, C., & Travers, E. (2009). *Making the most of interim assessment data: Lessons from Philadelphia.* Philadelphia, PA: Research for Action.

City, E. A., Elmore, R. F., Fiarman, S. E., & Teitel, L. (2009). *Instructional rounds in education: A network approach to improving teaching and learning.* Cambridge, MA: Harvard Education Press.

Danielson, C. (2005). Strengthening the school's backbone. *Journal of Staff Development, 26*(2), 34–37.

Darling-Hammond, L. (2009). *Thoughts on teacher preparation.* Edutopia.org.

Dorn, L. J., & Soffos, C. (2001). *Shaping literate minds: Developing self-regulated learners.* Portland, ME: Stenhouse.

Downey, C. J., Steffy, B. E., English, F. W., Frase, L. E., & Poston, W. K. (2004). *The three-minute classroom walk-through: Changing school supervisory practice one teacher at a time.* Thousand Oaks, CA: Corwin.

DuFour, R., Eaker, R., & DuFour, R. (2005). *On common ground: The power of professional learning communities.* Bloomington, IN: NES.

DuFour, R., & Eaker, R. (1998). *Professional learning communities at work: Best practices for enhancing student achievement.* Bloomington, IN: NES.

Evans, R. (1996). *The human side of school change: Reform, resistance, and the real-life problems of innovation.* San Francisco, CA: Jossey-Bass.

Fessler, R. (1995). *Professional development in education.* New York, NY: Teachers College Press.

Flaherty, J. (1999). *Coaching: Evoking excellence in others.* Boston, MA: Butterworth-Heinemann.

Fullan, M. (2001). *Leading in a culture of change.* San Francisco, CA: Jossey-Bass.

Fullan, M. (2007). *Educational leadership*. San Francisco, CA: Jossey-Bass.

Fullan, M. (2009). *The challenge of change: Start school improvement now.* Thousand Oaks, CA: Corwin.

Guskey, T. (1995). *Professional development in education.* New York: Teachers College Press.

Ingram, D., Louis, K. S., & Schroeder, R. G. (2004). Accountability policies and teacher decision making: Barriers to the use of data to improve practice. *Teachers College Record, 106*(6), 1258–1287.

Killion, J. (2008). *Assessing impact: Evaluating staff development.* Thousand Oaks, CA: Corwin.

Killion, J., & Harrison, C. (2006). *Taking the lead: New roles for teachers and school-based coaches.* Oxford, OH: NSDC.

Knight, J. (2007). *Instructional coaching: A partnership approach to improving instruction.* Thousand Oaks, CA: Corwin.

Krakauer, J. (1997). *Into thin air: A personal account of the Mt. Everest disaster.* New York, NY: Random House.

Lancaster, L. C., & Stillman, D. (2002). *When generations collide.* New York, NY: Harper Business.

Lovely, S., & Buffum, A. (2007). *Generations at school: Building an age-friendly learning community.* Thousand Oaks, CA: Corwin.

Marsh, J. A., Pane, J. F., & Hamilton, S. (2006). *Making sense of data-driven decision making in education: Evidence from recent RAND research.* Santa Monica, CA: RAND.

Marshall, K. (2009, Feb.). Mini-observations. *Education Week, 28*(20), 24–25.

Muhammad, A. (2009). *Transforming school culture: How to overcome staff division.* Bloomington, IN: Solution Tree Press.

Pace, E. (2009). *The X and Y of buy.* Nashville, TN: Thomas Nelson.

Pearson, P. D., & Gallagher, M. C. (1983). The instruction of reading comprehension. *Contemporary Educational Psychology, 8,* 317–344.

Popham, W. J. (2008). *Transformative assessment.* Alexandria, VA: ASCD.

Sarason, S. (1990). *The predictable failure of educational reform.* San Francisco, CA: Jossey-Bass.

Sax, L. (2009). *Sex differences are controversial.* Education.com.

Senge, P. (2000). *Schools that learn.* New York, NY: Doubleday Press.

Steele, J., & Boudett, K. P. (2009). The collaborative advantage. *Educational Leadership, 66*(4), 54–59.

Sweeney, D. (2003). *Learning along the way: Professional development by and for teachers.* Portland, ME: Stenhouse.

Sweeney, D. (2007). Mirror, mirror in the lab. *Journal of Staff Development, 28*(1), 38–41.

Warren-Little, J. (1982). Norms of collegiality and experimentation. *American Educational Research Journal 19*(1982): 325–340. EJ 275 511.

Webber, A. M. (2007, Dec.). Learning for a change. *Fast Company Magazine.*

Wheatley, M. (1999). Bringing schools back to life: Schools as living systems in *Creating Successful School Systems: Voices From the University, the Field, and the Community.* Norwood: MA: Christopher-Gordon.

Wheatley, M. (2002). *Turning to one another.* San Francisco, CA: Berrett-Koehler.

Wiggins, G., & McTighe, J. (2005). *Understanding by design.* Alexandria, VA: ASCD.

Wiliam, D., & Black, P. (1996, Dec.). Meanings and consequences: A basis for distinguishing formative and summative functions of assessment? *British Educational Research Journal, 22*(5), 537–548.

Index